To

Tha

Sup

how f you can go and there is no stopping you.

see you at the top girl.

Love Junior

HOW TO BE A STUDENT ENTREPRENEUR

Junior Oguneyemi

How to be a Student Entrepreneur

First published in 2011 by
Ecademy Press
48 St Vincent Drive, St Albans, Herts, AL1 5SJ
info@ecademy-press.com
www.ecademy-press.com

Printed and Bound by Lightning Source in the UK and USA
Designed by Neil Coe

Printed on acid-free paper from managed forests. This book is printed on demand, so no copies will be remaindered or pulped.

ISBN 978-1-907722-58-5

A CIP catalogue record for this book is available from the British Library.

Dedication

In my mind I painted a picture of someone reading this book and transforming their lives for the better. This picture is what spurred me on. So I dedicate it to you, the readers who are determined to make your dreams a reality… and I wish you all the best.

Acknowledgements

I never liked reading books as a child. I was the boy that would rather wait for the movie to come out before going to buy the novel. At one point I vowed never to read another book ever again. It was obviously a shock to many when I suddenly had the calling to write my own. I can only thank God that I didn't keep to my own will but followed His. I will forever be grateful for the grace bestowed upon me to complete this project.

Thank you Janell Owusu, my amazing PA who worked night and day with me doing extensive research. Your hard work has made the rich content of this book what it is. I appreciate your efforts and hope you are as proud of the impact this book has made on people's lives, as I am.

In everything I have ever decided to do, I know I have had the support of close friends and family who have cheered me on every step of the way. I honour my parents, Johnson and Grace Ogunyemi, and my older siblings. It's your words that I hold dearest to my heart. Thank you for speaking nothing but positivity throughout my life, and setting an inspiring example.

This book is the result of all the wisdom I have accumulated through studying the work of other bestselling authors, such as Robert T. Kiyosaki, Dr. Myles Munroe and many more great teachers. Thank you for laying the foundation to allow me to build on your work.

A special thanks to Vicky Pateman for your thorough proofreading and editorial skills. Your time spent on this has truly put the finest of finishing touches on the book. Thank you to Mindy Gibbins-Klein, Emma Herbert and everyone at Ecademy Press for supporting the concept and bringing my writing to life.

Last but certainly not least a big thanks to my mentor and brother Action Jackson who opened the doors and pushed me with a guiding and helpful hand. You poured every drop of greatness that you had to offer into me so that I could be the man I am today. I salute you!

Contents

Introduction

I trust you have been well trained to be an exceptional student. However the same may not be true as an entrepreneur. This is why the first part of this book is based on personal development, turning a great student into a great entrepreneur. I want to first inspire you to think, behave and feel like an entrepreneur before I give you the tools to go out and do it. As an entrepreneur, having the right character is what will make your vision, dreams and goal sustainable ones.

The second part of the book is where it becomes a lot more practical, showing you the ins and outs of business and how best to cope while still a student.

PART 1
Personal Development

CHAPTER 1

WHAT IS A STUDENT ENTREPRENEUR?

"IT'S A BIRD! IT'S A PLANE! IT'S A... STUDENT ENTREPRENEUR"

"Entrepreneurship is neither a science nor an art. It is a practice." *– Peter Drucker*

Welcome, ladies and gentlemen. It is with great pleasure that I announce there is a revolution coming! Very soon, there will be a time when CEOs of major corporations will be sitting at a desk alongside you, eating school dinners. There will be a time when somebody you know will have passed the million pound milestone before they have passed their driving test. I know this because, it has already begun.

All over the world, young men and young women with great expectations are secretly blossoming. By day, they might look just like typical, ordinary, college students. But by night, they are world changing, mini moguls. They are a new breed of super-humans. They hold the secret to success and true fulfilment. Each one of them has the power to dream into the future, and then make their vision a reality.

They have a level of determination and perseverance that mere mortals cannot even comprehend. In recent years they have been rapidly growing in numbers and are predicted to soon take over the world. Some describe them as ingenious, business starlets, future leaders or infant innovators. They call themselves STUDENT ENTREPRENEURS.

Is this book for you?

Being a student entrepreneur sounds fun, right? Well believe me, it actually is! Being an entrepreneur myself, I can testify it is the most wonderful way of earning a living. Nothing, except perhaps inherited wealth, provides greater personal freedom. Creating different streams of income for yourself not only provides financial freedom but also the freedom of time to do other things, such as pursuing your academic goals. You can follow your interests and develop yourself in any direction you choose. Free to live where and how you want, and to travel wherever the urge takes you.

Over the course of this book I will be revealing exactly how you can join the list of students that are already making their fortune before they graduate. Whatever you wish to study for, there is nothing wrong with making extra money with your own business venture on the side. This book is not aimed at encouraging students to quit school and start up business ventures. My aim is to inspire you with the necessary hope, ambition and nerve to give it a go, and to lead you through the various preparation stages so that you have a sensible, realistic plan and understanding of how to be a student entrepreneur.

Even if you consider business not to be your preferred career path, that's not a problem. There are still many valuable success principles a student entrepreneur knows, that you can apply while studying for whatever career route you choose to follow. There is definitely something in here that any high achiever will need to take on board.

Do you have the capacity?

Absolutely any student can become an entrepreneur regardless of their age or academic strength. Sir Richard Branson started aged 15, despite the fact that he was dyslexic. I recently had the privilege of meeting him at a business seminar. He openly joked that even at age 50, he sits in boardroom meetings with his financial advisors without understanding a word of what they are telling him. He revealed that at one point they had to draw pictures for him to grasp the concept of net profit and gross profit.

Sir Richard is a shining example of the magic an entrepreneur has. Despite all his limitations the genius is now one of the most respected multimillionaires of modern times. He is the founder of Virgin Records, Virgin Media, Virgin Atlantic and his latest venture to run commercial flights to space, Virgin Galactic.

I have had the privilege of meeting many different types of student entrepreneurs. Some are investors, singers, actors, lawyers, IT technicians and even proof-readers. The nine year old girl down the road that sells lemonade outside her front door is a student entrepreneur. All are making their fortunes learning how to set up ventures outside of the classroom, while still pursing their education inside the classroom. All display a form of entrepreneurial capacity.

I wouldn't want to sum up what a student entrepreneur is by reducing them to one sentence in a book. However, when I think about some of the incredible success stories I have heard and seen, a list of descriptions come to mind. Words such as *creative, determined, focused, passionate, bold, courageous, pioneer, extra-ordinary, successful, effective*… these are just a few ways to describe these young students. These are words that every student can and should be described as. In the coming chapters I will show you exactly how.

…creative, determined, focused, passionate, bold, courageous, pioneer, extra-ordinary, successful, effective…

NOTE: If you're somebody that does NOT aspire to become at least one of these, then you can stop reading now. Pass this book onto a friend.

BEST OF BOTH WORLDS

"Formal education will make you a living; self-education will make you a fortune." *– Jim Rohn*

Conflict or cohesion

I spend a lot of time studying the lives of many other famous successful people. When you hear the stories of people like Ralph Lauren, Simon Cowell, Steve Jobs, and Delia Smith it's easy to disregard schooling as important. All made their fortune despite dropping out of higher education.

It's now become a well-known misconception that to become a successful entrepreneur you must drop out of full time education, or to pursue an academic degree you must forfeit your other ambitions. Like many others, I am proof that the two can be managed if the right techniques are employed. In this book I will be speaking from personal experience and sharing a wealth of knowledge collected from other entrepreneurs. The aim is to challenge myths around the subject of being a student entrepreneur and share simple tips, techniques and resources on how to balance the two.

To do anything in life basic education is strongly recommended. An educated carpenter is more useful than an uneducated carpenter. The same applies for an entrepreneur. Education gives you more power and confidence as a business leader. Although experience is vital, being in education doesn't hinder your entrepreneurial hopes. There need be no conflict between the two. The truth is you can use your student status as a greater advantage.

Never a better time

Learning how to use your student status to your advantage as an entrepreneur will certainly get you further. Enjoy the best of both worlds. The skills and discipline you learn from your study will prove invaluable when pursuing your entrepreneurial venture. Tasks like meeting coursework deadlines, waking up early, group presentations are all common practice in business.

There may be particular topics from your course that you are studying that can also apply to your venture. I constantly applied theories I was learning from my psychology lessons to understand how to get the children I was coaching to behave better. We learn much better in school if we experience things, as opposed to just reading about it in theory. Being able to practice and draw on real life experience of what your class is studying may even boost your grades.

Lower risks

One of the big fears about entrepreneurs is that they are too risk-loving. Well, if this is true then what better time to start taking the risk than as a student. Let's face it; you haven't got much to lose. Most of you will not be tied into a permanent job. Most of you will not be tied into a mortgage. Most of you will not have a spouse and five kids that you must provide for. Just about the hardest decision most young people make is, "what should I say in my next tweet?"

I meet so many middle aged employers who have only just decided to get their feet wet in the entrepreneurial pool but can't. At their age the risk is far greater than when they were students. They now have to consult their spouse, or consider the bills that are flooding through the door. The longer you leave your dreams on hold the greater the burden of risk becomes.

Access to networks

As a student you have so many opportunities available to you. When I started university I was told that I would be joining a group of 9,000 other students on campus. Instantly pound signs started flashing in my head. I figured that I had just been handed a 9,000 member-strong customer base. If I could sell something for as little as £2 each to every member on my campus, that would be £18,000 income. This was more than enough to pay my rent and buy my first car.

The types of people you will meet are also a big help. I became friends with so many incredible people during my time at college and university. Many of these friendships proved useful when I needed cheap labour or resources for my business. In fact, whatever I wanted I knew someone who knew someone who had an uncle that would help out.

Access to resources

Schools are probably the best place when it comes to resources. As a student of any institute you have free access to their libraries, computers and even printers and office equipment. Make the most of it.

You also have access to teachers who are likely to be experts in particular topics. When I wanted to start an online business I went to and consulted a law lecturer before going through with it. He was able to give me tons of advice. Had I not been a student I would have had to pay huge hourly rates to get the same advice from an independent lawyer.

Access to funding

As a student you also get grants, loans and pots of funding literally thrown at you in abundance. The sad thing is most students do not even realise or bother to search for it. In most countries the student loan is one of the lowest interest rated loans available. If you invested that money into a business or even moved it into another account with higher interest you could make a nice profit by the time you finish education.

Greater publicity

Possibly the best part about starting off as a student is that everybody loves to see a kid do it. Juggling footballs looks cool, but it's much more fascinating to see a five year old do it. The same attention, respect and fascination is granted to a student entrepreneur.

During university I won over 10 different awards, and

featured in several magazine headlines, most of them simply for being young! The publicity you will get provides great exposure for your business. Older entrepreneurs that have finished higher education cannot share the same luxuries.

When it comes to making your millions and fulfilling your dreams, there really is no better time than as a student. For me, learning to get the balance right was so useful. It gave me assurance that even if my business ventures did not work out the way I planned, I would always have a great education to fall back on. This book will teach you how to manage your time, stress and business in perfect harmony so you can truly enjoy the best of both worlds.

A CANDLE IN THE DARK

"Success is not in what you have, but who you are"
– Bo Bennet

I salute you!
On a more personal note, let me congratulate you for picking up this book, and I salute all those that will actually go forth and apply the life changing principles it contains. I have endless respect for the people who will truly dare to live their dreams and demand more for their life.

These are the people that know their worth. Entrepreneurs carry a fearless aura that is contagious. Playing small is unattractive. They are not afraid to dream big. They are not afraid to fail. They can live with failing, but they cannot live with never even giving it a shot.

In today's economic climate I anticipate more students will realise there is not as much security in the job market, and will be seeking to start up their own ventures or just create another stream of income before they graduate. These are the smart ones that are not relying on the approval of an employer to decide how far they can go in life. They are not over-reliant on the examiners' marking criteria to decide their financial future.

The world is waiting

Due to the rising cost of school fees, I also predict that the growth in demand for young people wanting to learn how to be more enterprising will continue to rise dramatically. More and more student entrepreneurs will emerge. They will be the cause of the next economic boom. They will be the saviours of the unemployment crisis. They will be the financers of future investments. Student entrepreneurs create intellectual and financial wealth where everyone can benefit. The success of these high achievers will be the source of comfort for impoverished communities around the world. Their ideas will be improving the way we live and learn.

This is why I describe student entrepreneurs as super-humans. This is why I salute you who have chosen to join them. We live in a time of transition where the systems and institutions we so heavily depended on are crumbling. You are the future leader that will restore trust in society.

By fulfilling your dream and starting a successful venture, you will be the new hope. With so much need for entrepreneurs you will be an unstoppable force, you will deliver the solution to our problems. You will be our candle in the dark.

CHAPTER 2

REVOLUTIONISE YOUR MIND

The age old saying "you are what you think" is still very much applicable today. To become a student entrepreneur, you must first learn to think like a student entrepreneur. Everybody in life wants to maximise their potential. We all want to be more, do more and have more. The student entrepreneur is no different.

You want to get the good grades, pursue your passion, keep in touch with friends, meet coursework deadlines, manage your company and make your own money etc., all without feeling stressed. As impossible as it may seem, this can actually be your reality.

However, in order to be more, do more and have more success in all areas of your life, it will require a higher level of thinking. To maximise your potential and become that student entrepreneur you must revolutionise your thoughts. This chapter will show you how simple it is.

THE EAGLE MIND-SET

"For as he thinketh in his heart, so is he" – Proverbs 23:7

What is the eagle mind-set?

This is the fundamental component that separates the student entrepreneur from the rest of the class. The eagle mind-set is a thinking pattern of a champion that reflects the student entrepreneur's determination, courage and success.

Eagles are astonishing creatures. They are one of the most powerful birds of prey, and all the other little birds know it. When hunting, an eagle can spot its prey from roughly two miles away. When a storm arises the eagle doesn't run for cover, but rather uses the wind from the storm to generate air lift, which then allows the bird to fly above the storms. The eagle flies at a much higher altitude than most other birds. Where human beings can only see three basic primary colours, the eagle's vision is so sharp it can see up to five.

The eagle's actions are fearless and focused because of its mind-set. The way the eagle is exceptional compared to other birds is the same way you, the student entrepreneur, must be exceptional compared to other students.

Is the eagle mind-set really that hard to obtain?

This eagle mind-set is one of the most valuable skills a person can have. The sad fact is that very rarely is this mentality taught in the classroom, so we grow up unaccustomed to it. Neither would you be able to find the eagle mind-set in society, because society is full of average people aiming for mediocrity. Average is defined as being the best of the worst, and the worst of the best. You are greater than that, and you know it!

The situation has caused many to fall into wrong believing, so when we do come across that individual who is an exceptional achiever, we seem to think they were just naturally made that way. There is no success gene. The truth is this mind-set is not a gift that only the few elite students are born with. It's a nurtured mentality available to all. This is simply a higher perception of yourself that anyone can develop, regardless of your academic capability, race, religion, social status or gender.

Accessing that untapped potential

Although you rarely find this skill out in the classroom, or out in society, you can find it hidden within yourself. Just for a second try not to be "realistic" or "down to earth". Do not focus on your flaws or limitations. Look deeply into how much untapped potential you have. Think of how good you can be at that subject if you put in more hours of work.

Rather than asking yourself "what happens if I fail?", try to imagine what your life will be like if you succeed. Once you practice getting into this higher frame of mind, you will be flying into a whole new realm where you believe all the things you want in life are actually possible.

Every day you should focus on how much potential you have in you. Did you know that if you sacrifice that hour of extra sleeping you do, it will accumulate to seven hours in a week? Over the course of a year you could have tapped into an extra 15 days. How fluent would you be if you used seven hours a week to learn a new language? Or you could have used that time to learn to play a new instrument. If you consider the theory of six degrees of separation, you are only six phone calls away from having an interview with absolutely anyone you want. This is how much potential you have in and around you.

Are you an eagle that has been conditioned to live in mediocrity?

One of the things I get so frustrated about is that we are all capable of doing more. However, we are limited by our own thoughts. Imagine an eagle that has the power to fly at a high altitude parallel to the sun but does not believe it. It has the strength to pick up prey three times its body weight but is too afraid. This is an eagle that has been conditioned to live in a mediocre way instead of seeing the greatness that dwells within. That is more like a chicken mind-set.

> ***"Logic will get you from A to B. Imagination will take you everywhere."*** *– Albert Einstein*

Open your mind to greater levels of reality

I have met many successful people and they all share the same belief. They do not perceive reality from a negative stand point. Reality to them is whatever they choose to make it. One person's reality may be completely different from what you perceive it to be. Once you remove the limits that your rational mind places on you, you will begin to tap into the eagle mind-set and dream big and at a higher altitude.

I never believed it was realistic for a person to achieve eight A* grades in their GCSE exams. That was until I met a girl who did. This instantly opened my mind to greater levels of what reality is. I used to believe making money was a hard painstaking process. This was before I saw a man make over £400,000 within seven minutes right before my very eyes. All these experiences opened the door to what is really possible, and my perception of reality moved from a mediocre level to that of a high achiever. The more I choose to expose myself to these incredible people and experiences, the more I am creating a new reality.

There is no entrepreneurial gene

One key fact that I will reiterate is that there is no entrepreneurial gene. This means we can all easily develop it. Nobody has ever been born with the innate ability to see great opportunities, have the confidence to execute business deals, manage or freeze time so that a hundred things can get done all at once. However, there are a group of people who seem to be doing just that.

The children of billionaires are more likely to become self-made billionaires even if you take away their inheritance. This is not through their genetic make-up, but because of the way their mind has been trained. If you could tap into the same lessons and principles of a billionaire's mind-set, what's to stop you from also becoming a self-made billionaire?

BECOME AN EAGLE

***"Eagles fly, chickens fry"** – Action Jackson*

One of the best ways to think like an eagle is to actually behave like an eagle. I don't mean you should grow a beak and go sit on a nest of eggs. However, I will cover two distinct behaviour patterns that eagles display which could help reshape your thinking to develop that eagle mind-set.

- ***Eagles spend most of their time flying solo***

Very rarely would you see a picture of a flock of eagles. Every image I have of eagles is that of one soaring through the clouds, commanding the skies on their own. Eagles are not afraid to go it alone. Unlike other species of birds they don't mind leaving the security of the flock and finding their own path.

To become a student entrepreneur, you must get used to flying solo. Don't be like sheep and follow the herd. Most of the great leaders of our time are those who went against the trends of social norms and created their own paths. We commend people that do this because it's not easy. For young students in particular, this seems like one of the hardest things in the world because at some stage peer pressure governs their life. We all have some level of peer pressure that we succumb to.

Get used to breaking free

This is the only way you can truly be yourself and transform into a student entrepreneur. While all your friends are out raving, you're going to need to finish that coursework assignment. While all your friends are running scared of the lack of jobs available in the economy, you're going to need to think outside the box and write business proposals to create new jobs. At first it will feel lonely and awkward, but you're training your emotions to fall in line with the eagle mind-set.

I'm not saying you should cut off from all friends and lock yourself in solitary confinement. No way, that is extreme. But at the same time do not get stuck at the other extreme where you think exactly like your friends, you make the same decisions as your friends, behave exactly like your friends, because this will only lead to the same results as your friends.

You will regret the past time wasted following the flock

As you practice flying solo, soon enough it will not feel like something you have to do, but more like something you want to do. Once you see how much happier and productive you become, you will regret the past time wasted following the flock.

At the end of the day, you will always learn, the group of people you are trying to impress now will not be with you forever. Those peers that you so loyally followed, who influenced and shaped your decisions, are never there later on in life when it is time to face the consequences of those decisions. They have moved on. They have graduated, changed cities, chosen a different career path, gone on to live their own dreams.

If you were to catch up with the flock 10 years from now, you'll find that they will no longer be the same. Some have joined new flocks, others have made the choice you should have made and gone solo. It's your life; you make of it what *you* want, not what your social group wants, not what your parents want, not what the media tells you to want.

- ***Eagles wait... then soar effortlessly***

A different technique to flying

Have you ever observed the flight of a duck, or a pigeon? If so, you should have always noticed the exasperating way they flap their wings. This is not just during take-off but also throughout the entire flight. Did you know eagles hardly ever fly like this? When you look at an eagle it is usually soaring gracefully and effortlessly without even flapping half as much as other birds. Before an eagle takes off, it will sit still, waiting on the mountain top with its wings stretched out wide. It holds this position, continually waiting for several hours if needs be. As odd as this behaviour may seem, it is actually quite genius. What is the eagle waiting for… wind!

Waiting on the winds

The mountain top is where the winds are greatest. The eagle's out-stretched wings act as a gauge to measure the strength of the wind. Once the eagle feels the wind is strong enough it takes off by leaping from the mountain top and using the lift from the strong winds to carry it to its destination. Effortlessly!

This is why eagles hardly ever waste energy flapping around like other birds, but glide gracefully and more quickly through the air. This is also what allows the eagle to fly at heights of over 1000ft., an altitude most other birds could only dream of reaching.

I speak to many young people who tell me they have plans to be famous. Once I ask them why they want to be famous they reply with a simple, *"I dunno, I just wanna be"*. There is no wind in their plans. They have nothing that will seriously motivate them to outperform others. This is why when they face barriers in reaching their goals, they easily quit.

What or who is your wind?

What gives you the strength to reach your destination? What are you depending on to carry you through? Like the eagle it would be wise to wait on your winds to come before you decide to launch. For some people this could be a prompting from God. Or it could be a high calling such as helping children in third world countries. Maybe is it the promise of a job offer or hope of a scholarship.

I know some entrepreneurs that reveal their ultimate driving force is the happiness of their children or loved ones.

This is what gives them the extra strength to get up in the morning and keeps them encouraged to do what they do, and perform at the highest altitude possible. Whatever your winds are, make sure they do the same.

> ***"Mother love is the fuel that enables a normal human being to do the impossible."*** *– Marion C. Garretty*

Recap

So as a student entrepreneur you must start becoming more eagle-minded, and the easiest way to think like an eagle is to act like one. Learn to fly solo and develop a better technique of flying by using the strength of your strong winds. You are now well on your way to mastering the eagle mind-set.

There are a few other simple techniques and tools you need in order to completely revolutionise your thinking into that of a student entrepreneur.

REDEFINE YOUR WORDS

> ***"Whatever it means to you will determine what power it has on you."*** *– Junior Ogunyemi*

Words have a powerful influence on our thoughts. Therefore, in order to revolutionise your thinking it would help to redefine negative words.

Words to actions cycle

A positive word can evoke positive thoughts that generate

positive emotions, which is the fuel for positive action. This then leads to more positive words, thoughts and emotions… so the cycle continues. Unfortunately, this reinforcing feedback loop is also true for negative words. Too many times we hear negative words such as "failure", or "loser". This conjures up negative thoughts of being worthless, or below average. Your emotions quickly respond to these thoughts, and you begin to feel down and miserable.

Effect on your physiological state

Even when you try to hide it, often your physiological state would give it away. You may slouch, or perhaps walk around with your head hung low. Your voice even goes quieter. For that period of time, or until new thoughts come into your mind, you are no longer in a peak state and will constantly be performing below your best. This is how powerful words can be. So be careful next time you start using negative words so loosely.

Do not allow negative words to change your productive state

It's inevitable that people will criticise or speak badly about you or what you are doing. We are trapped in a world where negativity is the norm. Even in the media it's a well know saying that "bad news sells". Although it's hard to prevent yourself from reading, hearing or speaking negative words, one effective method of stopping these negative words from affecting your productive state is to change the meaning you attach to them.

Failing my driving test

When I started taking my driving tests, there was a period when it seemed the letter F was the only letter in the whole alphabet my driving instructor could write. Every test centre I went to, every car I drove in, my instructor would always award my driving ability a big fat F for "FAIL".

For a while it seemed I couldn't get away from hearing

the word. Whenever my class mates asked me how I did on the test, I had to answer, "I failed". Whenever I had to fill out application forms requesting my score on the previous test I had to write down "failed". Although I tried to forget my failed attempts it became a constant reminder, and gradually shifted me from a peak state to the point where I wanted to give up on driving.

That was until I made the decision to redefine what failure meant to me. So I wrote down the equation, "failure = feedback". This was the new positive meaning I attached to the word. It created a more optimistic approach to taking my driving test. Every failed attempt now meant even more feedback for me to go and improve.

I'm sure my driving instructor thought I was crazy every time I started rejoicing when he told me I had failed once again. But I really didn't care; to me, hearing that I had failed now meant I had discovered more areas to improve on so the next attempt would be flawless. After 6 attempts at my driving test and hundreds of pounds given to the DVLA, I finally passed. Even better, I did it in style with practically zero minor mistakes.

Had I not made the decision to redefine that familiar word "failure", I probably would not have had the resilience and hunger to repeatedly go back until I eventually got what I wanted.

We all have our own perception, use it to your advantage

To many people it may seem odd that you choose not to perceive certain words in the same way as the rest of society. However, even when there is a social norm as to exactly what something should mean, each individual still has a slightly deviated perception of what words mean to them.

If I was to say the word "dog" some of you may picture a cute furry animal. On the other hand, the word "dog" to someone else could mean a dangerous scary beast. There are even probably some who hear the word "dog" and think of their ex-partner.

Your emotions will show in all areas of your life

As a student entrepreneur you must have and maintain this resilience. You must keep positive at all times to be at your best. If you allow negative thoughts to kick-start negative emotions, your actions will show in all areas of your life. I know a girl that went through a bitter break up with her boyfriend and this started to not just affect her future relationships, but also her grades and her business.

Rather than seeing the break up in the negative form, I told her to view it as "I'm finding 'me' time". Instantly she wasn't so reluctant to talk about her ex-boyfriend. She no longer operated in a negative state. She made better decisions and things started to change around for her. She spent more time going out on dates, treating herself to shopping sprees and planning her future. In her mind 'break up' now meant something exciting, a release, something fun to look forward to.

What are your negative words?

What triggers your negative emotions of worry, self-pity or depression? How can you change the meaning to something that is more empowering?

If you are still finding it difficult to re-define what words mean to you, then why not try to use different words to express yourself? For example, no matter how hard things got financially I would never confess that I'm "broke". Success talk for "broke" is… "I'M OVERCOMING A CASHFLOW PROBLEM". Try it starting today; see how negative-proof your mind becomes.

THE S.W. ATTITUDE

"If you don't like something, change it. If you can't change it, change your attitude." *- Maya Angelou*

The worst three hours of my life

When I was 17 I had the privilege of working very closely with another businessman and esteemed motivational speaker known as Action Jackson. I had previously attended many of his seminars and they were truly life changing. As you can imagine, such a dynamic speaker had been generating much interest, and due to popular demand he had planned to host a huge event titled, "LIVE YOUR DREAM". I was so excited that I even offered my assistance with the preparation. I had no idea what I was letting myself in for.

I expected to be asked to come up with a great marketing campaign, or creative ideas for the poster design. However, I became stuck with the most demoralising task of all. I had to hand out flyers to passers-by on the street. It was too late to back down now. I reluctantly picked up my stack of 300 flyers and headed for the busiest part of town to catch rushing passers-by.

After three hours of standing in the rain, I had only successfully given out a pitiful nine flyers, three of which were scrunched up and thrown back at me, and one which was used by a woman to scrape her dog's mess off the floor. It was possibly the most humiliating three hours of my life, with over 2,000 rejections and enough dirty looks to last a lifetime.

I became so frustrated; by the end of the day I was ready to quit this job. I didn't mind not getting paid but I did mind having my self-esteem crushed to smithereens in the record time of three hours. I marched back into Action Jackson's office to hand back my stack of unwanted flyers so I could leave, go home and cry.

This was when he pulled me back, shut the door and happily confessed that he sent me on the most humiliating assignment deliberately. I grew even more frustrated and my attitude turned sour. I couldn't understand what I had done to deserve such treatment.

"If you already knew how much I hate rejection, why would you send me on such a task?" I questioned. It made no sense to me. That's when he sat me down and began to reveal the secret of the SW attitude.

He told me, "If you want to become an entrepreneur you must change your outlook to the one that every successful person has. You need to have an SW attitude."

Some Will, Some Won't, So What! ....Someone's Waiting

Whatever product or service you offer the world, you will face rejection. It's inevitable. But you cannot take it personally. The more you let it get to you, the more rejections you will get. What I needed to do was change my attitude. I had to understand that some people will want the flyer. Yet some people won't. So what! Whether they do or they don't, it's not the end of the world.

Regardless of your outcome, keep going in the hope that out of all the 6.5 billion people in the world someone is waiting for that flyer. Through it all just remember that what you have to offer is just what someone, somewhere is waiting for.

In the end I decided to go back out on the street the next day equipped with my new carefree SW attitude and the remaining flyers. I'm proud to say I managed to distribute almost 70% of the remaining flyers. Result!

A man trying to please everyone is like a dog chasing its tail.

Whatever you do in life will never get a unanimous thumbs up. So What! Don't get carried away by those who love you, don't get down by those who reject you. This is my message which is vital in order to overcome obstacles on your road to greatness. If you fail to apply anything else you read in this book, please make sure you keep the secret of the SW attitude and use it when applicable. Some will like your ideas; some won't like your ideas... So what!

Take hope from the knowledge that someone is waiting for it. Someone is waiting to see your movie, someone is waiting to hear your song, someone is waiting to read your book, someone is waiting to read your CV. Someone is waiting for a person with your skills to walk through the door and accept their job offer. So do not give up regardless of all the rejections.

PRACTICAL APPLICATION

Task 1:
Get out a sheet of paper; divide into two halves by drawing a line down the middle of the page. On the left hand side write down three negative words or phrases that you have ever heard in the past, or may hear regularly. These could be anything that pulls you down from your peak state when you think about it.

Now opposite this on the right of the page, write down a new empowering meaning that you can attach to the negative word. Look at the word or phrase in a different light and see how it can benefit you. Below are three examples.

E.g. if you're a marksman at a shooting range hearing the phrase:
"Missed the target", change this to mean
"need to re-aim"
This creates a more optimistic thought towards missing. Re-aiming gives you hope that you are improving, so you should try and have another go.

e.g. "FEAR", change this to mean
False Experience Appearing Real
This new meaning gives you boldness knowing that whatever you are fearful of is just an illusion.

e.g. "hard work" changes this to mean
worthwhile work
Now every time you hear someone describe an activity as hard work, you will not be discouraged because to you it will now mean there is something about that activity that is richly rewarding, whereas other activities that are not hard seem worthless.

Now think of another three words or phrases of your own that you can work with.

CHAPTER 3

FINDING THE MILLION DOLLAR IDEA

We spent the previous chapter building a key foundation, which is the student entrepreneur's mind-set. Everything you picked up in chapter 1 will make you better equipped for doing what is required in all the other chapters. In this next chapter, I will show you techniques to become someone that can easily generate million dollar ideas.

"Business opportunities are like buses, there's always another one coming." – *Richard Branson*

Now it's time to capture and build upon your thoughts to generate fantastic ideas. There is a saying that at least once a year everyone gets a million dollar idea. If this is true then you may have missed out on many great ideas in the past because you dismissed them too soon, lacked knowledge of how to develop them or probably didn't even realise you were onto something. Whatever the problem was we are now going to fix it.

Why call it the million dollar idea?

Although most ideas will probably not make a million, we still refer to it as a million dollar idea because every idea has the *potential* to make a million dollars, pounds, euros, yen, naira… remember, as entrepreneurs we only focus on the greatest potential something has.

So why do most ideas fail?

Personally I don't believe businesses fail because the ideas were weak; I think it is because the execution was weak. Who would have thought the idea of a talking sponge that lives in a pineapple under the sea would take over the world? As ridiculous as the concept of SpongeBob Squarepants is, the execution was brilliant.

It has now expanded to the point where SpongeBob and his friends are on TV all over the globe; sell their own merchandise; have made a movie; and the square pants sponge even has his own clothing line, for adults as well as children. The moral of the SpongeBob story is that you should not be too quick to dismiss any wacky idea. With the right execution every idea has some potential.

Be passionate

Starting a successful new business takes time. So as you begin to think about compelling new business ideas; remember, none will bring you more joy than those based upon areas in your life where you are most passionate. If you're going to invest the long hours it takes to plan and successfully run a new business, it is better for you to do that in something that gets you excited. When you find something you love doing you will never have to 'work' a day in your life. Your passion naturally translates into every aspect of your business.

If you lack passion for the new business, your planning effort will almost certainly be stunted. Dispassion about your business will ooze out in nearly every area of your business – making it even harder for you to attract investment funding, hire good employees and earn revenue. In a competitive marketplace, dispassion can nearly condemn a new business to failure even before it starts.

ADDING VALUE

"Successful people are always looking for opportunities to help others. Unsuccessful people are asking, what's in it for me?" *– Brian Tracy*

Ideas make the world go round. Money just tags along for the ride

If you're desperately searching for ideas and regularly find yourself mulling over the same question in your head, "what will make me a lot of money?", then I've got news for you. You're asking the wrong question! What you should be asking is, "where or how can I add value?"

When I tell other aspiring entrepreneurs about this, many of them brush it off as if the whole notion of adding value to people's lives is some airy-fairy philosophy from the tree of life. Well if that's the case then one thing I'm certain of is that this airy-fairy tree of life produces the best fruits. All the greatest ideas throughout history were discovered there.

Where is the fame? Where is the financial fortune? Where can I make a name for myself? Such questions take your focus away from making ground-breaking discoveries. Indeed, all the money and fame may come along, but only as a by-product of having a great idea that actually adds value.

Facebook story

When Mark Zuckerberg birthed the concept of Facebook his focus was the entertainment value that the site provided to its users. Even as the company grew bigger and bigger, this remained the primary focus. All the changes they made to Facebook since its birth have been innovative ideas based around improving users' experience on the site. This approach has generated many ideas that are now opening up multiple streams of income for the company.

Where would Facebook be if they didn't seek to add value?

Let's imagine we were back in February 2004 when Facebook had just launched. Mark Zuckerberg and his team are in their Harvard dorm rooms hanging onto the wrong school of thought, *"what will make us money?"* Can you guess the type of ideas they would have come up with to improve their site?

When I tried this exercise two of my first thoughts were to either charge users, which will generate more money quickly! Or maybe to make the interface smaller so they could have more advertising space to sell, also generating more money quickly!

I'm afraid to say back in 2004, I doubt anybody would have been interested in signing up to a social networking site that hardly anyone used yet, and which had a small interface filled with other unwanted internet adverts. To make matters worse, imagine the company expected you to pay for the service when there were already a host of other free sites available. If money-making was the only thought in their mind, I don't believe Facebook would have seen anywhere near the 750 million users that it has today.

Both of the above ideas were great money-making strategies but would have failed terribly because they missed the focus. In order to make money you must attract customers; to attract customers you must add value to them in some way or another. The two ideas above add very little, if any, value to users, or other companies that Facebook would do business with.

Wherever you look around you, there are people adding value to their service or product. This is where your ideas should be centred. This could be in the form of how to make something easier for consumer to use, make things faster, make things cheaper, make things more eco-friendly...

Chinese restaurants vs. Chinese take-away shops

Take the example of the plush up-market Chinese restaurant and your local backstreet Chinese take-away shop. Have you noticed that the special fried rice you eat in both is practically the same? The sweet and sour sauce is the same, the noodles are the same. However, the Chinese restaurant can happily charge you three times the price of the take-away.

This is because you are not paying for the meal; you're paying for the restaurant's environment. You're really paying for the cool air-conditioning, the comfy seats, the waiter escorting you to your table, the mellow background music while you eat. The up-market restaurant took the exact same product you find in your cheap back alley take-away and found creative ways to add value to it. In doing so, customers feel like they are getting a better experience and the restaurant earns considerably more revenue.

So overall, adding value to other people's lives is not just beneficial to society but even more so for the student entrepreneur. Practice this way of thinking. There is nothing wrong with wanting to maximise profit, but the best ideas in doing so only come when you learn to take your eyes off the financial gain. Only then will you come up with more creative, quality and successful business ideas.

STOP MOANING, START LISTENING

"An entrepreneur trains their mind not to look at problems, but to look at solutions." - *Junior Ogunyemi*

A negative norm

In order to generate great ideas you first need to learn how to stop moaning! An entrepreneur is not a victim. Things don't happen to you, but rather, you make things happen. In today's society people love to moan about things; the weather, their bosses, the TV, the internet speed etc. Moaning is a negative approach to life, which breaks the entrepreneur out of his/her peak state.

The effects on your creative mind

To grasp great ideas you must remain in an interested peak state about everything you come across. When you are constantly nit-picking you are sending messages to your brain that, "things are never right". Your mind, spirit and body will eventually respond with the following phrase, "Your wish is my command". Everything from them onwards becomes one big moan after another.

Whether you are aware of it or not, when you moan you are gradually training your mind. Over time you are turning your creative mind into your very own fault-finding friend. This now becomes the voice that looks for all the faults and problems in life. But when you shut up and stop moaning you begin to see the hidden gift in every problem. You no longer automatically notice the faults in things, but start to find solutions. That's when you have struck gold!

Problem solving is the job of every type of entrepreneur

Choose to be the one who doesn't join in with the moaning because through that you only ever become an expert at moaning. Rather than joining in, listen to what problems the rest of the world is complaining about and see that as an opportunity to solve them.

The Happyfeet story

I recently heard about a company called Happyfeet that are becoming one of the most talked-about brands today. The story behind Happyfeet is a perfect example of a young entrepreneurial mind solving an age-old problem that other mediocre minds have been complaining about for decades.

I'm sure most females can relate to the feeling of going for a night out clubbing in high heels. You dance the night away for hours and by the time you're ready to go home your feet are absolutely killing you! Walking home in bare feet is an option, but cuts and dirty feet don't really appeal. Rather than joining in with the rest of the complaining girls, one lady decided to solve the issue and design comfy fold up shoes that can fit into any handbag. Thus Happyfeet was born. Girls were now able to purchase shoes that they can slip on once the party stopped and make their way home without the pain.

I'm sure the founder of Happyfeet wasn't the first to

experience this problem, but she managed to do what every successful entrepreneur does and develop an idea that brings the solution to what everyone else is moaning about. Instead of playing the moaner, start playing the listener, that's when you can spot great opportunities.

YOUR THINKING ENVIRONMENT

***"It's important to determine which surroundings work best for you, and then build that environment to suit your needs."** – Marilu Henner*

At this stage you should have understood what to do and what not to do when searching for ideas. You must look to add value, and must not get stuck or trapped into a moaning mind-set. Now your ideas are heading in the right direction to get that million dollar eureka moment. In this section I will show you how to create the best environment for an idea to be birthed and flourish.

The eagle's nest must be a safe place

Eagles build nests when preparing to give birth. These nests are usually secure places, quietly tucked away in the corner of a mountain. You must also find the right environment to birth your future. Make sure this birthplace is kept secret and secure away from predators. You may be on to a good thing and you do not want to give it away to the wrong people. Protect your babies.

It's a good idea to always carry a small journal or notebook with you to jot down your thoughts. Don't start posting your big ideas on Twitter or Facebook. Only show it to those that you can trust and those who you need on board, i.e. mentor, business partner etc. Openly sharing your undeveloped thought with the world is like an eagle laying its nest in the middle of traffic on a busy city street. It will quickly get crushed. While you are still in the developing stage keep it between you and your journal as best as you can.

Keep your ideas away from dream killers

Some people may not even wish to steal your ideas, but they can still kill your dreams by quickly dismissing it for you. Once you spill the beans on what you plan to do, someone always comes up and says, "You can't do that"... "You're too young"... "You're too inexperienced," etc. You then find you were better off keeping most of your thoughts private. I call these types of people dream killers.

Your mind is now revolutionised into that of a student entrepreneur, unlike their mind which is still stuck within the confines of a mediocre society. To reach the top you must, and will, always dream bigger than others do. So obviously, you going around sharing your thoughts with them is a big mistake. Either they will get offended that you even have the audacity to believe you are greater than average, or they will laugh at you because it doesn't seem realistic.

Always hold a notepad and pen

Another benefit to having a notepad and pen on hand is that you never forget. Going back to the notion that everyone gets a million dollar idea at least once a year, the worst thing would be to forget yours and have to wait another year.

Ideas can pop up at the most random of times - maybe when you're out swimming, cooking, watching a movie, eating a burger. Wherever you are, whatever you're doing, always have a pen and notepad handy. Other alternatives could be using the note-taking function on your phone or I-pad.

What's your favourite spot?

I have a friend who claims that his best ideas come when he is sitting on a toilet. This sounded odd at first but now I have become used to it. Every time I invite him over to my house, he may visit my bathroom several times in one night.

When he enters armed with a pen and notepad I know exactly what he is going in there for. If he doesn't leave the toilet for another 30 minutes, I can only imagine he is onto something big. Indeed, this is strange behaviour to some but I don't complain about it anymore; he is an incredible student entrepreneur and that's just his favourite spot. By having his notepad, pen and a quiet enclosed space where no dream killers can poke their nose in and interrupt, he has successfully created a perfect thinking environment for himself.

It's better to have the internet close by

Personally I like to sit alone on a quiet window ledge and look out of the widow with my pen, notepad and sometimes my laptop. That is my environment. I keep my laptop on hand so that I can quickly look things up on the internet and do my research while I'm thinking.

Sometimes I am trying to come up with a catchy name for a company, and when I find one I like I will usually type it into Google to find out who is using it, or to check if the idea that I thought of has already been taken. With the internet now accessible on almost any phone, researching your ideas wherever you are has become much easier.

Use creative stimuli

Another method is to have a special room in my house where I can work. I place funky creative furniture in this room to trigger my mind into thinking and looking at things creatively. This is my creative stimuli. Rather than chairs I may have bean bags, on the walls I have fun paintings, a coat hanger shaped like a giraffe, and on my desk a goldfish bowl shaped like a huge brandy glass. These are just some of the things that help me to think outside of the box.

I also have a scribble wall where I write down what's in my head, draw animations and graphs. Once I have exhausted all my ideas I step back and look at the huge mess I created on the wall. This usually forms a big mind map, so when I'm developing my idea I keep looking back up at the wall to get inspiration or decide what comes next.

Now I must warn you. Before you start getting carried away with writing on walls, I suggest you get permission from the owner of the house.

Having a peaceful setting

I mentioned I like to stare out of the windows, but I do not do this to find my answers. I already have the idea I'm working on in my head. However, the beautiful view of the clear sky and clouds quietly drifting around helps me clear my mind; I get rid of all the clutter deposited by other people, events or news that may be running around in my head. Once I have a clear head I can focus better and quickly jot things down when they come to me.

You must find or create your own environment. This needs to be a place where you come to quietly meditate, relax your mind and get creative. Make sure you are comfortable, but not so comfortable that you doze off.

DIVERGE THEN CONVERGE

"No idea is so outlandish that it should not be considered with a searching but at the same time a steady eye." *- Winston Churchill*

There is a special technique that the best student entrepreneurs use when brainstorming. It's described simply as "diverge then converge".

Step 1: DIVERGE

You begin by writing down every little thought that comes to mind. Literally, write down everything! Regardless of how insignificant, stupid or unrealistic it seems, write it down! Let the ideas flow and drift out. Do not stay focused on the topic, feel free to stray. This is the first part to proper brainstorming.

At this stage do not dismiss anything. If you are brainstorming as a group, the team leader must not judge anyone's idea yet but accept all contributions. Nothing that is proposed gets rejected when diverging.

Dig deep

The whole point behind this is to get a deeper quality and larger array of answers. The first few ideas that people usually come up with in a brainstorming session are the obvious ones that are on the surface. Once you have spent 10 minutes scratching the surface, your mind usually appears to go blank as if you have run out of ideas.

This is the point when you add an extra five minutes to dig even deeper. Push yourself to think of more ideas. What you normally find is that the ideas in the last five minutes are deeper and of better quality. It's similar to going to the gym; the first few reps on the dumbbells are easy. The truth is you are not actually building anything. It's only once you reach that pain threshold that your muscles begin to really pump and grow. This is not the time to stop. Keep going and push yourself for another four reps.

Step 2: CONVERGE

The next stage from here on is when you begin to pull your thoughts in. Now you can converge back to the focal topic and cross out each idea, one by one, after thorough examination. You can keep some of the obvious ideas and you may find some of the not-so-obvious ideas useful. One by one slowly pick off the ideas that won't work or fit into your plan. Eventually you will bring your thoughts to a conclusion. The last few ideas standing will safely be the most creative and most feasible.

The problem with the way most people explore ideas is to dismiss the not so relevant things straight away. People who brainstorm like this are basically converging first, which is the wrong order. This never works because when they later try to diverge they quickly find themselves limited with ideas to play with. They leave no openings to think outside the box. What they normally find is that the quality of their idea is much weaker and their solutions just don't match up to that of an entrepreneur.

FIND A MENTOR

"If I have seen further it is only by standing on the shoulders of giants." – *Isaac Newton*

Tap into the minds of great thinkers

To get greater ideas, you must think like those that are already greater. There's no better way of doing so than by having a mentor. The opportunity to learn from those who are well respected experts in a particular field is something every student entrepreneur should relish. Whatever level you are at, you will always benefit from having a mentor. Your road ahead could be very long without one.

Rome wasn't built in a day, but there are people out there who have built Rome and most are more than happy to show you the blueprint. People love to talk about themselves. They will be able to show you things from their experienced perspective. A good mentor will reveal pitfalls that they fell into and shortcuts that they discovered. This will help you build and shape your million dollar idea better. One thing that holds most people back is fear of the unknown. The guidance of a mentor will give you a better picture of what lies ahead and more confidence in going forward with your idea.

A mentor does not necessarily need to be someone who is older than you

When choosing a mentor, remember experience is better than age. It's more important that they have done or are doing what you intend to do. If you are considering going to university to study a law degree, look for others that have already taken modules you will be doing. Find out who got the highest grade in the previous year. Track them down. Get their old notes. Ask questions about what aspects of the course they found easy and what they found hard. This will place you a few steps ahead of the rest of the class. If you're able to meet with your mentor over a cup of coffee, then that would be even better. Through building up a genuine friendship you're more likely to adopt their thinking pattern.

Tracking down a mentor

Tracking down someone whom you would like as a mentor is easier than you think. You may bump into a managing director of a big organisation at an event. Look for an opportunity to network. Introduce yourself confidently. The initial introduction would not be the best time to start firing your endless list of questions. However, you can make it your simple goal to get their business card.

Within 48 hours of meeting your potential mentor, make sure you contact the person via phone call or a quick e-mail. You must do this within 48 hours, otherwise they may forget who you are. If you met them at a networking event then your chances of being remembered are even slimmer. As you can expect, your potential mentor would have shaken hands with another 30 others that same night.

When you decide to call or text simply say something along the lines of:

*"Hi, **XXXX** it was a privilege meeting you the other night at **xxxxxx**. I'm currently working on a project about **XXXXX** and would value someone with your expertise to mentor me. Would you be able to meet up sometime next week?"*

Find out where their favourite restaurants are and offer to take them out for lunch. Once the date is set have your pen and paper ready to take notes and ask questions. Try not to impose or be too personal too soon. Like any relationship it needs time to build trust. If you found the first date useful then see if the two of you can arrange more time in your schedules to make the learning lunch a regular thing.

The mentor and mentee relationship need not last forever

You may move from one mentor to another mentor depending on how fruitful the mentorship has grown to be. You may also have several different mentors at the same time. I have many mentors that help me with different areas of my life.

I have faith mentors, business mentors, finance mentors, even a gym mentor who makes sure I stick to my daily workout. Each mentor is a specialist in their specific field so I get the best advice and guidance in all areas of my life. As I continue to learn more from these people I start to get more ideas coming to me.

Martin Luther King Jr. mentored me

I often meet many people who tell me they want to do something great but don't have anyone they can contact who will be a suitable mentor. I tell them that in the past I have had the privilege of being mentored by great minds such as President Barak Obama, Napoleon Hill and even Martin Luther King Jr. I have never once met these men face to face. Nevertheless, I have tapped into their minds; I have seen the world from their perspective and used their way of thinking to get better ideas.

How can you do the same? Read books written by, or about, other great thinkers. Look up articles on people you admire. Spend time studying videos of them sharing their thoughts in interviews. The internet is so amazing that I can find out detailed information about any individual or company within seconds.

Libraries are full of people who have spent 60 or 70 years of their life making mistakes, and they have summed up all the lessons learned in one book for you to read. Make it part of your day to study great thinkers. This is all part of your daily routine of spending quality time with your mentor. If you were meeting your mentor for coffee you would write it in your diary because it's important. Learn to do the same when it's time to read up on great thinkers.

Key questions to ask

If you do have the privilege of meeting up with your mentor regularly, below is a list of general questions you may want to ask.

"What do you do?"
"How do you do it so well?"
"How did you get started?"
"Why did you get started?"
"What setbacks have you experienced or mistakes have you made along the way?"
"How did you overcome this?"
"What have you learnt?"
"How have things changed?"
"Would you advise that I go about it this way…?"

PRACTICAL APPLICATION

For the next two weeks you will be retraining your brain not to spot problems, but rather to look for solutions.

1) Over the next two weeks monitor your behaviour. Every time you find yourself complaining about something, donate 50p to charity. It will be almost like having a swear jar. Fine yourself for dwelling on faults. This will help retrain your mind not to dwell on problems. It will all be for your own benefit in the end, so do not cheat yourself! Find a good friend or a mentor that can be accountable for your behaviour.

2) Carry your journal with you for the two week period. Although you can't complain, you can keep an eye out for when others do. Whenever someone you meet is moaning about something write it down. This could be absolutely anything. i.e. *"the service in this restaurant is too slow"* or *"my hairband keeps falling off"* etc. Write down anything and everything you hear from friends, family, radio, TV...

3) Once the two weeks are up, look back at how much moaning you did. There should be a gradual decline over the two weeks. If so then congratulations, you have begun retraining your brain. If not then start all over again and increase the fine from 50p to £1 per complaint.

Also look back at your journal and by the end of the two weeks you will hopefully have pages full of complaints from other people. This is your gold mind for ideas. In your hand you will have a list of problems that need to be solved. Using this list as a starting point, go into your thinking environment and start developing solutions for them.

CHAPTER 4
TIME MANAGEMENT

If you want to know the value of an hour, ask the mother that only gets an hour to see her son in prison. If you really want to know the value of a minute, ask the man who, after a long day at work, missed the last train by one minute. If you want to know the value of a second, ask the Olympic runner who missed out on a medal by one second.

In order to set up your ventures successfully while studying, you must learn how to manage your time. Time management is so vital that I have dedicated a whole chapter to it. If you don't learn how to give yourself enough time you will end up falling behind and panicking. Time is probably the most precious endowment you have. Until you start having a new-found respect for your time you will never be able to achieve the greatness you aspire to.

CHOOSE YOUR PERSONAL PRIORITIES

"You do not have enough time in life to do everything, but you do have enough time to do the important things."
– Junior Ogunyemi

What is important to you?

I can tell how important something is to you by looking at how much time you invest in it. If you spend more time playing video games like Call of Duty than you do studying, then you're more concerned about your points earned on the game than you are about the points scored on your next mid-term exam. This is the simple truth. It may not be the way you want to be, and it may not be the way things are supposed to be. However, that's just the way it is.

Until you stop being in denial about it and make the conscious decision about where your priorities are, things won't change. Sometimes we need to stop and analyse who or what we are giving most of our time to. This will be an indicator as to what results you will be getting. Those who are serious about investing in the future and become financially free will make their business venture one of their top three priorities.

Hope and ambition

What are your dreams and aspirations? What are your goals as an entrepreneur, as a student, as a boyfriend/ girlfriend etc? These are an indication of where the majority of your time should be allocated to. Anything else that is not in line with your aspirations should be considered a waste of time.

If I plan to get a 1st class degree, and know I have my final exam in two days. I should spend the majority of the next 48 hours doing things that get me closer to that goal. 90 minutes watching the Chelsea football game over the weekend has no bearing on my long-term goal of a 1st. I do not get extra marks on my science exam for knowing who scored what goal. As much as I love watching Chelsea, this should be considered a waste of time for the next 48 hours at least.

Define your inner personal talents

Another indication of where your priorities should be is in your personal talents. If you want to become a student entrepreneur but lack the know-how, time spent reading this book should be a priority. Why? Not just because I'm the author, but also because you will be building your knowledge, which is taking you closer to those plans, dreams and aspirations.

Any time spent developing areas that you are weak in is a good idea. It's an even better idea if they are areas that are important to your future. Define the inner personal skills you're going to need for your venture, your studies and future life goals. Write down a list and honestly rank each by how strong you are in it. You may have good computer literacy skills but not so good people skills. Start working on your people skills. Poor people management and lack of communication could be a major barrier to you being successful in the future.

PEAK PERFORMANCE TIME

"Much may be done in those little shreds and patches of time which every day produces, and which most men throw away." - Charles Caleb Colton

There are normally particular periods or moments of the day when we are most productive. Use these peak performance times to do the most difficult task on your list. Below is an indication of when and where peak performance times may arise.

- **Minimal distractions** - if you love to watch TV, make sure it is off. Also if you feel that the internet may distract you make sure you turn it off in order to make your work/studying effective. Some people live in households with others who always bring distractions. Work around their day, get most of your work out the way before your little brother comes home and blasts on the TV.

  If you are totally into video games, social networking sites or DVDs, discipline yourself to only enjoy them after you have finished your studying as a reward. Perhaps get them out of sight, give them to a friend who will only return them once they have seen how much work you have done that day. Every minute that you are away from distraction, is a productive minute that can be used.

- **Your study/work environment -** Good lighting and temperature is essential. If it's too hot it will be harder to concentrate, so it's better if the temperature is a little cool. Comfortable chairs will allow you to relax and prevent back aches. The more time you spend in the right working environment the more productive your time will be, as opposed to sitting at a desk for hours just daydreaming.

- **Time of day during which to study** - choose a set time of the day that you feel comfortable with. If you work well during the day make sure that you wake up early. If you are a night owl set out a time in the evening to study. If you know your business relies on constant communication with partners it may be a good idea to respect the 9am-5pm business hours that every other business operates under. Even if you are a night person, calling up suppliers at 3am won't go down well.

- **Take regular breaks-** It's a well-known fact that people are at their most productive when taking regular short breaks. A good routine is to totally focus, 100%, for at least 40 minutes at a time – then take a five minute break. Don't study for too long otherwise the body and brain will become tired. Study for at least 40 minutes and then take a short break. If you are doing a task that you really enjoy you could probably stretch this.

PLAN YOUR TIME

"Finding some quiet time in your life, I think, is hugely important." *- Mariel Hemingway*

Being prepared for the day is much better than being unprepared. Little things like having planners, diaries or other devices to structure your day save so much time. Ideally you want to be able to own your time, and do not just what needs to be done but also have time for what you want to get done. It all starts by planning where your time is going to go.

Be prepared

Gather all the information and materials needed for your assignment. This saves time. The most frustrating thing would be to break a productive session because your pen ran out of ink. Have several pens available. Have your books ready and open to the pages you intend to cover.

The better you are organised means the better your time is organised.

Checklists and daily to-do lists

Timetables are a good visualising tool that allows you to set times for when you start and finish work.

Having a daily to-do list not only helps you plan your day, but also helps you remember what should get done. I find the best method is to have a list of the tasks that need to be done written down in order of priority. This means I always get the most important and urgent tasks out of the way first.

Try not to allocate a specific timeframe to each task. It never works. You either end up running over or finishing earlier than anticipated, in which case you will end up with too many time gaps to loiter in, or you end your day with a bunch of unfinished projects.

Don't rush the job. However long it takes you, spend your time and focus on that particular task. It's normally the important jobs that are most time-consuming but also require the most focus. Even if you do not finish all that was on your to-do list, at least the most important tasks would have been completed because they were started first.

As you are completing each task, make sure you tick it off on your list. It is scientifically proven that humans get a sense of satisfaction when they cross something off on a list. Whenever we mark something as completed our bodies release endorphins which is the hormone that makes us feel happy and fulfilled inside. So keep crossing off those tasks and releasing those endorphins, it's good for you!

Reduce non-essential time

Make a list of the things that are real time-wasters, such as having casual chit-chats with your friends. Cut down on the unnecessary things like watching television. If you read magazines a lot you can rip out the articles that are necessary to you.

By eliminating or combining the non-essentials you can save so much time for more important tasks. If you're on your way home to do some work and you bump into someone that wants a chat, why not suggest they share their world while they walk you to the station?

Here you are combining your time to do both and putting a limit on how much of your time they take from you. We have all been victims of someone who ask us to spare five minutes, then all of a sudden when we sit down with them, the conversation turns into 30 minutes, which then rolls into an hour. This is all non-essential time that could be used getting the important things done.

Recuperation is key

You do not work best at all hours of the day. To prevent

illnesses and stress related problems make sure your body and mind have enough time to rest. The seventh day is known as the day of rest, which seems quite coincidental because our bodies work on a seven-day cycle. Traditionally, when you are sick or have a virus the doctor usually tells you to rest, then they come back to examine you after seven days.

Rest is just as important as work. See it like charging the battery to your phone. We always get in a panic over how many things we must get done in so little time. However, you will be able to get three times the amount of productive work done if you just rest once in a while.

Break down major tasks into smaller tasks. Allocate pause times into your schedule. Switch off your phone once in a while. When people ask you to do work during your breaks, tell them you are far too busy doing the most important task of the day.

Plan for problems

Always plan some leeway within your planner because problems can arise. However you plan your day it will never ever go 100% perfectly. The bus will not arrive the exact second you anticipated, not everyone will show up at the meeting on time, little things may slip your mind. Rather than letting these things ruin your schedule, plan for them.

USING TRANSITION TIME

"Time is what we want most, but what we use worst." *- William Penn*

Using unproductive time

Unproductive time is any period of time that you are using doing things outside of your priorities or things that are not directly constructive for your overall goals. Unproductive time itself is not necessarily destructive. It just means time that is not allocated for working directly towards your ultimate goals. For example, if my goal is to finish a first draft of a business plan, waiting for the kettle to boil is unproductive time.

Periods of unproductive time are unavoidable. When it occurs in between major tasks it is often referred to as unproductive transition time. The journey from one classroom to another classroom is usually unproductive transition time. Now you need to start thinking of ways you can turn this unproductive transition time into productive transition time. How can you make these short periods between tasks work in favour of achieving your ultimate goals?

Examples of transition times:

- *Journey to and from school or college*
- *Waiting for people to arrive for meetings*
- *During breakfast*
- *Waiting for appointments*

Cutting down on transition time is always helpful. Make one less journey and try to do two things at once. This will enable you to save time. For example, while you pick up the laundry walk the dog as well. It saves you having to make two trips wandering the streets.

If you can't cut down your transition time then find a way to make it productive. These time slots can be filled productively, whether it's by reading a book or following up on some unfinished school work, for example dropping off a book at the library and also doing the dry cleaning. This prevents one from making the journey twice.

Below are a few more tips on what transition time can actually be used for to make it productive transition time.

Use your transition time to:

- Catch up on reading
- Make all those important phone calls
- Make notes about the projects or assignments that are given to you
- Meet people
- Take a nap
- Exercise
- Plan out what you will do later
- Organise your notes
- Get some "me" time

Next time you are sitting on the bus, rather than listening to music for the whole journey make this transition time a productive one and get some of these little but important tasks done.

CONQUERING PROCRASTINATION

"Procrastination is like a credit card: it's a lot of fun until you get the bill." *- Christopher Parker*

What is procrastination?

Procrastination is the art of putting off doing something. The more times you put things off until the future, the harder your future will be. It's even more dangerous when major tasks are being put off. The lack of consistency in getting things done straight away can be very costly.

Procrastinators sabotage themselves. If time is the

most valuable commodity you have, then you should want to create more of it, not waste it. Some forms of procrastination even seem constructive. Have you ever sat down to work or study, then told yourself you can't work until your room is tidy? You then spend a whole 40 minutes tidying your room, even though you would never normally be bothered. This is procrastination at its best. Even though you are doing a good thing, you are not doing the right thing.

Why we procrastinate

It is easy to let procrastination become a habit rather than a once-in-a while thing.

Reasons may include:

- Fear of failure

  Most people put off tasks they feel they will not perform well at.

- Boredom with the task

  You may need to make a task more stimulating to prevent yourself falling victim to procrastination.

- Lack of time

  The perception that you do not have enough time to complete the task causes you to postpone the whole job until tomorrow.

- You haven't defined your goals

  You are not yet clear on what you want to achieve or you feel the goal is not yet strong enough to motivate you to get it done.

- You've got other problems worrying you

  When issues outside of the task play on your mind, it affects your emotional state which then affects your actions. This is why it's important to remain in a peak state.

How to tackle procrastination

- Start now

  If you're given an e-mail to forward do it as soon as it arrives. If you're given coursework deadlines, start as soon as the assignment is handed out. Even if you feel you have all the time in the world to do it later, other tasks will always get in the way. Start now! Get it over and done with as soon as it arrives.

- Define exactly what needs to be done

  Make the vision or targets clear. Before starting write down how much you intend to get done, and why you want to get it done. Even though the "why" may seem obvious, it helps to constantly remind yourself.

  Perhaps another good thing to write down is what it will cost you if you do not get this task done. Scare yourself a little. Stick the answers to this question up on your wall as you are working. Whenever the desire to procrastinate causes your eyes to wander, you will see the target that should rekindle a greater desire to keep working until it's finished.

- Divide the workload

  Tackle the job in small steps in order to spread out your time evenly and produce your best work. If you need to read a particular book, don't try and do it all in one night. Target a chapter a day. You absorb more of the book and you remove the fear of not being able to complete it all at once. Get giant tasks down into little bite size pieces. Complete each piece one at a time.

  Breaking the workload down also helps the quality of your work. By getting each little bit right first time you save hours of having to go over correcting errors. Try to work steadily through the small steps needed to complete the task.

- Prioritise the tasks to be done

  Once again prioritising is vital. It helps sort out the things that get you closer to your goal from those that don't. See above section on "choosing your personal priorities".

- Reward yourself

  Once you know that you have completed a large amount of work and you know that you have worked to the best of your ability, give yourself a reward. It could be something small like a chocolate bar. Rewards give you motivation to continue to repeat the same behaviour.

RULES TO GOVERN THE CLOCK

"Time = Life, Therefore, waste your time and waste your life, or master your time and master your life." - *Alan Lakein*

In this section I have highlighted the key tools required to control your time better. Below is a summary of what I have covered plus more useful tips. Bookmark this list and make sure you're practising them on a daily basis.

1) **Preparation is key**
2) **Prioritise your tasks**
3) **Deadlines are helpful to aid your organisation**
4) **Give yourself a reward**
5) **Use timetables and checklists**
6) **Eliminate as many interruptions as possible**
7) **Send away visitors, they can result in little actual work getting done**
8) **Leave time for corrections, review and collation**

9) Ensure that all parts of the job are complete
10) Get it right first time
11) Correct your work as you go along
12) Remember not everybody is perfect, we are not ROBOTS
13) Make sure that you have the right positive attitude when doing your work
14) Having a negative attitude does you no favours, no matter how mundane the task may be
15) Do not be late - lateness can have serious consequences
16) Arriving early is no crime
17) Learn the art of delegating
18) Make use of time-saving technology such as, dictating machines, laptop computers, electronic notebooks, Voice recorders

PRACTICAL APPLICATION

1) If you have not got one already, buy a timetable.

2) Get a sheet of paper, write down the following five questions and stick them on your work desk.

WHAT IS GREAT ABOUT THIS TASK?
WHAT WILL I AND OTHERS STAND TO GAIN FROM COMPLETION OF THIS TASK?
WHAT IS THE LONG TERM AND SHORT TERM COST OF NOT COMPLETING THIS TASK?
IS THE TASK COMPLETED ON TIME AND TO THE BEST OF MY ABILITY?

Always run through these questions as you are doing any task.

CHAPTER 5

STRESS MANAGEMENT

In this chapter I will be talking to you about stress and ways to cope with stress. As you know stress is part of life, but it is most prevalent in fast-paced societies. However, stress is not always bad. A good student entrepreneur needs stress in order to set goals and achieve these goals. So when stress is actually beneficial it is called "eustress".

Nevertheless, there are times when stress is overwhelming; in this case it is called "distress". Instead of being beneficial it can harm you. Therefore an important part of an entrepreneur's healthy lifestyle and wellbeing is to learn how to cope with stress and get results under pressure.

UNDERSTANDING STRESS

"Adopting the right attitude can convert a negative stress into a positive one." *- Hans Selye*

What is stress?

The definition of stress is the body's physical response to a perceived demand or threat.

Advantages of stress

Like I said at the beginning of the chapter, stress is not always a bad thing. All good student entrepreneurs welcome stress because it has its advantages. The stress response is the body's way of protecting you. When working properly, it helps you stay focused; giving you extra strength to defend yourself, the stress response also helps you rise to meet challenges. Stress is what keeps you on your toes during a presentation within schools and universities, sharpens your concentration and drives you to study for an exam when you'd rather be watching TV.

Before you start reporting to the clinic for stress pills, know which type of stress you're working under. Here are a few clues to spotting the different effects of the different forms of stress.

Eustress - People can work well under pressure as it motivates them into reaching their full potential.

Distress - People tend to have nervous breakdowns or may become depressed.

There are two main components to stress.

1. There is the mental component which is the perception of stress;
2. Then there is the physical component which is the body's response to stress.

For stress to occur there must be a perception of a threat or a demand. This happens when the person feels they didn't have enough resources to deal with the situation in an effective way. These resources normally include:

- Time
- Money
- Energy
- Patience
- Intelligence
- The support of others

The key point here is ***perception.*** It doesn't matter if the reality is different. If a person feels that they are lacking or don't have all these resources, they will experience stress.

MISPERCEPTIONS ABOUT STRESS

There are two common misconceptions:

Certain situations are naturally stressful because of their excessive demands

This is not true. Because there is a general consensus that a particular activity is stressful, this doesn't mean you must automatically submit to a state of stress. For example, going on tour around the world for five months may be a stressful experience to some musicians. However, others actually find it the most peaceful time and use the opportunity to write new music.

A lot of stress is linked to how we see things and our mind-set. This is why I spent the first chapter shaping your mind so that your perception of a situation would be different. In an economic crisis where everyone else is panicking, you can remain cool, stress-free and notice the new opportunities the crisis creates.

Stress depends on our biology - genes and hereditary factors

Stress consists of both physiological and psychological factors. The psychological part involves our cognition, the way in which we input and output information. This will have a greater impact on your performance than anything else.

Just because your parents were stressed, doesn't mean that you are doomed to a life of high blood pressure and stress. Your parents faced different situations to you and they had a different frame of mind. The only reason a child develops the same stress-related illness as their parents is because they choose to handle situations in the same way their parents did.

SEVEN COPING STRATEGIES

I have highlighted seven key steps you can take to ensuring that you are taking on less stress. The first four are possibly the most effective. If you can manage to achieve these four your chances of beating stress will increase considerably.

- **Have a strong support network**

  Your support network includes people like your family and friends. It's always good to have people around you that you can turn to or talk things out with. Whether they give you good advice or not is a different issue, nevertheless having a sounding board is helpful because you pour out all the stressful thoughts from your mind.

- **Your sense of control**

  Having a better sense of self control over a situation helps to keep things calm. Did you know that most people show greater anxiety when travelling on a plane, than they do about driving? This seem irrational when you consider that statistics show you are more than 20 times more likely to have a crash in a car than you will on a plane. However, people are still calmer about driving because they know that they are in control of the steering wheel.

  Anything you can do to increase you influence on a situation, do it. It will bring you peace of mind.

- **<u>Your attitude and outlook</u>**

  We have spoken about attitude a lot in previous chapters. Staying optimistic is a vital ingredient to making a success of anything. The mind-set and attitude of an entrepreneur is what propels them to be so great. Each and every day, regardless of how things appear, see yourself getting the desired result one way or another.

- **<u>Your knowledge and preparation</u>**

  The more you know about how long you will be in a stressful period the easier it will be to cope; for example, knowing that exams last for a set amount of time and realising there is a worthwhile end result.

  The more knowledge of the situation you have is also linked to how much control you feel you have. The same is true for how prepared you are. Prepare to prevent things going wrong. If problems do arise, find out as much about them as you can.

- **<u>Practice 4 A's - Avoid, Alter, Adapt, Accept</u>**

  AVOID - stressful people, conversation, situations as best as you can.

  ALERT - alert yourself when you know that there is a potential threat if something becomes too stressful. You may be able to solve the issue before it gets out of your control.

  ADAPT - Your mind and body are so powerful that they have the ability to adapt to almost any stressful situation when they occur. Some people find that starting a new job that requires them to wake up at 6am is stressful. Eventually the person's body clock will adjust to the new sleeping pattern so it feels less stressful.

Rather than getting your boss to change your work hours, it may be better to let your mind and body change. Allow this process of adaptation to occur.

ACCEPT – When there are things that you know you definitely cannot control, just let it go i.e. realising you wrote the wrong thing after the exam has finished. Worrying won't change the circumstance at this stage. You can stop carrying the burden of stress if you accept certain things the way they are.

- **Get a massage**

  Your body reacts to a stressful state. Through massages you relieve the tension stored in your body. As the body is relaxed, it sends messages to the brain that the stressful situation is over. This is why your mind returns to a state of peace when your body is relaxed.

- **Take at least one good holiday a year**

  Escape the situation by changing your environment. Short breaks away are well deserved for the entrepreneur that has been battling through many stressful circumstances. Even when the stressful situation has passed, things in our daily environment are a constant reminder of the stress that we previously faced. Book a flight to your favourite holiday destination and unwind.

PRACTICAL APPLICATION

One of the biggest issues with busy people is that when they get home and fall asleep their mind keeps over-running like clockwork. Our mind hates cramming things in. When you write down a phone number your mind doesn't need to worry about remembering it. If you do not want your head filled with stressful thoughts, write things down.

1) Every night before you go to bed, write down on a sheet of paper all the things you need to remember for the next morning, i.e. pick up your granny, call the technician, complete the application… the more things you write down the fewer things your mind feels it needs to remember. This will allow your sleep to be much more peaceful.

PART 2
Getting down to business

CHAPTER 6

A BUSINESS STRUCTURED FOR STUDY

Before you go all-out to start your money making venture make sure you know how it fits into the plan for your life. You will need to decide how you will structure your venture so it will not interfere with your study demands or other areas of life.

Many students find it far too difficult managing a business while at university so they opt to take a year out. This may sometimes be the most sensible option as you have more time to fully focus all your energy on the business. However, it need not be the only option. There are certain types of business that can be structured easily around your study timetable. This means you can focus on the two and perform exceptionally well in both. The secret to doing so comes from understanding that it's not just about how hard you work, but how smart you work.

THE TRAP

How did I fall into the trap?

When I started the football coaching academy, we were based in a small area in north London. This was our first and only location for three years. Everything was going fantastically, we quickly reached full capacity and the business was maturing steadily. When I was entering to my final year at university I planned to allocate more time towards study. After all, the business was going perfectly just the way *I* wanted it.

However, that was the problem. Everything worked around 'me'. I was the head coach, managing director, accountant, salesman, admin officer, PR officer, and even the coffee boy. Although I had a great team of people working with me, I realised all the systems had been built around me and my expected schedule. So when it was time to change my schedule I became trapped.

I had made the same mistake that many enterprising students make. Because the business was built around me, when I wasn't around the business wouldn't be around. I began to realise that I couldn't even take a holiday. If I went on holiday the business had to go on holiday until I got back.

The more the business grew and expanded the harder I had to work. Because I fell into the trap, the blessing started to become a curse. As we generated more publicity, schools started to call us in to run coaching sessions. I was forced to turn some down because I couldn't be everywhere at once. I became the key component for the business to operate.

All this resulted in less time and energy for my studies. I began working much harder trying to balance my work and study. Although I would give myself full marks for hard work, I knew this was not working smart.

A mistake I see happen all too often

Many people call themselves entrepreneurs but they are not. They are just people that are enterprising. There is a big difference between an entrepreneur and someone who is enterprising. If you are not clear on the difference you are more likely to fall into the trap.

An entrepreneur is a business owner, whereas the person who is enterprising is self-employed. The entrepreneur spends time working ON the business, whereas the person enterprising spends time working IN the business. As the business grows the entrepreneur can generally spend less time at work and more time doing other things. On the other hand, when business is growing for the person enterprising, they must work even harder.

An example of someone enterprising would be the ice-cream van man. Or the independent graphic designer that creates artwork for clients by himself. If they take a day off, the business takes a day off. This is because they work in the business. On the other hand entrepreneurs build systems that run by themselves, which means that profit is being made regardless of whether the individual is around or not.

I must point out that there is nothing wrong with enterprising, especially if you are doing something you love. For example I quite enjoyed coaching football so did not mind working overtime doing it. However, to be successful as a student entrepreneur I would advise you to be less enterprising. For the rest of this chapter I will be showing you how to set up your business the smart way so you don't fall into the trap.

OWNING A P.I.G.

The smartest way to avoid falling into the trap of overworking yourself is to turn your business into a P.I.G. as quickly as possible. The acronym P.I.G. stands for **P**assive **I**ncome **G**enerator. This is a business that operates well without the entrepreneur directly participating. The business can generate a profit without your on-going work input. The most successful student entrepreneurs are experts at this. They structure the business to run on autopilot.

This is how I solved the problem I was having with the rapid growth of the football coaching academy. Turning the business into a P.I.G. allowed me to have more time to focus on studying while the business kept churning money. I did not need to take any gap years to focus on the business. Neither did I need to shut down the business to focus on studying. Best of all, I was able to take as many holidays as I wanted whenever I wanted.

I became completely free to reschedule my life any way I desired without harming the growth of the business.

To enjoy the same freedom to study and run a business you must structure your business correctly from the start. This means not around you, but around other systems that are independent of your involvement. In the next few sections I will introduce you to commonly used structures to having a business that involves less of you.

OUTSOURCING

One of the best structures to help cut down on your workload and create more time is to outsource. Outsourcing (also known as sub-contracting) refers to the system of contracting out work to a third party.

Spend less time, get better quality

Not only will outsourcing save you time, you are more likely to get the work done at a higher standard of quality. The individuals or organisations that offer to take on the workload for you are usually experts or professionals in that field. For example, hiring a trained accountant to manage my finances means the job would be done faster and more accurately than if I were to do it myself.

When a building is being constructed, outsourcing becomes a major deal. A general contractor may take care of a number of tasks, including the brick-and-mortar construction, but look to sub-contractors for other types of tasks, especially things like plumbing and electrical work. These disciplines are nearly always sub-contracted out. The general contractor does not have the time, skill or resources to do such tasks. The same principles often apply to building a business. There may be many aspects of your business that are better suited to be carried out by people who have the time and expertise required for that task. Pay them to do it so you don't have to.

This is what many successful ventures operate. Entrepreneurs do not know everything. But they do know how to hire skilled workers to get the job done for them.

How I set up a business without lifting a finger

During my second year at university I started a publishing company that produced different genres of student magazines. Along with running the football academy and studying for an economics degree I knew I didn't have time to fall into the trap. I didn't have time to be editor-in-chief, salesperson, distributor, marketing manager etc. So I decided to adopt the outsourcing strategy and literally outsource everything.

I divided the publishing company into three major sections: production, distribution and sales. These were the three most important areas that were required for the publishing company to operate. I placed them at high importance because they were the most time consuming and operated inter-dependently.

Once the production team had produced a good quality magazine this then had to be mass produced and delivered to customers by the distributing team. For customers to pay for the magazine it needed to be marketed and publicised. This also attracted advertisers that would pay the sales team for advertising space. Part of the revenue collected by the sales team was then given to the production team to produce the next issue. Then the cycle continued. This was how I planned for the system to work in my mind. The next step I took was to find suitable people and companies to do each task.

Production sub-contracted

I first gathered a strong editorial team to work on production. This meant recruiting graphic designers, proofreaders, creative editors, content editors etc. Managing a production team can be time consuming so I hired an editor-in-chief to manage and oversee all the activities of the production. The editing team could produce a much better magazine than I could because they were specialists on the topic. For example, if it was a fashion based magazine I ensured everyone involved in the production were fashion fanatics. They knew what appealed to the target market better than I did.

Distribution sub-contracted

I went online and found a company that posts leaflets to people's houses. I then outsourced the distribution by hiring them to take copies of the magazine to specific locations and distribute it. I only met and spoke with the manager that was in charge of the distribution. He gave me regular feedback and advice on how to improve because he was a specialist at distribution.

Sales sub-contracted

I then sub-contracted the sales to an advertising agency. They pitched the magazine to potential advertisers and sold advertising space. This was our main source of revenue. For every advertising space they sold I paid them 20% commission. They had the contacts, sales team and time to make far more sales than I could ever do on my own so sharing 20% of the revenue was a far better deal.

The end result

In the end, I only spent about a month setting up three key systems and outsourcing the tasks to specialists. Once systems were in place, everything moved on by itself like clockwork. The production team were busy producing the magazine, the distributers were getting the magazine out to people, and the sales team were generating profit. There was nothing left for me to do. I had successfully created a passive income generator.

A high quality magazine was being produced, delivered and making me lots of money without any on-going input from me. Occasionally I met up with the managers of each department to get an update on how things were going or feedback to them how I wanted things to be done better. However, overall I was left with far more time to focus on studying. In total I had a team of over 50 individuals across three departments that were working for me on the project, even though I had never met any of them face to face. I only ever needed to deal with the managers of each department. They would then relay my thoughts and plans onto their respective teams. The fewer people I had to manage, the less stress I had. Working smart!

Advantages and Disadvantages:

Before deciding which route to go down it's important you fully understand the pros and cons of each business structure.

Advantages

- You can outsource tasks when you need more **flexibility**
- You can use outsourcing for one-off jobs and jobs that require specialist **expertise** or a fast turnaround
- Your permanent staff can **concentrate on the core business**
- Some contractors / sub-contractors can start the work or project at **short notice**; even when large numbers of workers are required they will already have the resources to complete the job
- You can obtain temporary **cover** for a permanent staff job or work that needs doing

Disadvantages

- Sometimes outsourcing may **cost** your business more than the equivalent daily rate for employing someone
- By relying on contractors / sub-contractors, your business **does not acquire or develop skills** in-house
- **Permanent staff may resent** others being paid more

money for doing similar work to them

- If you use a contractor that then uses a sub-contractor, you have no direct control over the **quality** of the sub-contractors' work
- The people you outsourced your workload to may not appreciate your business culture and may lack the **motivation** and **commitment** of permanent staff

MLM

Another time-saving business structure is to join an MLM company. MLM refers to Multi-Level Marketing which is a marketing strategy that compensates you for joining their sales force. In most MLM organisations, you will not only earn commission for your sales but also for the sales of others that you recruit. This creates a down-line of distributors and a hierarchy of multiple levels of compensation.

How MLM works

When you join an MLM organisation there is usually an initial joining fee. You will then have access to the business systems and can set up your own outlet selling the product. A friend of mine called Emma once joined an MLM company that brought out a new innovative video e-mailing technology. This was their product. Every sales person in the company would sell the use of the video e-mail technology to customers.

For my friend to join she paid as little as £200. Emma then became a registered sales representative for the company. For every product she sold to someone she would receive a percentage of the revenue earned. This was one stream of income for her; however, it couldn't really be considered as passive income because she still needed to put in a lot of effort to sell. Spending hours cold calling is not something a student entrepreneur would have time for.

Working smart

Now if Emma chose to recruit me as another sales rep this would open up more streams of income for her that didn't interfere with her time. First of all she would have received a percentage of my £200 joining fee just for recommending the company to me. Also she would have received a percentage of every product I sold. This would have been on-going income for her as long as I remained a sales rep within the company. So she could have simply sat back and focused on her studies while she earned residual income from the fruits of my labour.

Working even smarter

What is even better is that if I were to recruit my friend Steve into the business I would have got exactly the same deal. Emma would then be given a percentage of revenue earned by Steve and myself. If Steve went on to recruit his friends the pattern would continue throughout the chain of sales reps.

As Emma was at the top of the hierarchy she would be earning the most passive income while spending the least amount of time on the business. This is a very effective way of structuring a business for your studies.

The business systems are already in place for you to use

Another huge benefit of MLM organisations is that you don't need to worry about setting up business systems, designing a product or even racking your brain for an idea. They already provide a product for you to sell and an easy business system to use. This means that your success rate in this business structure is a lot higher, especially for those that are novices when it comes to business. This structure is more feasible than others in terms of its practicality.

MLM companies are usually designed so almost

anyone can join and run their own selling outlet. If you were to start up a business from scratch there is always the risk of not having enough assets, not knowing or managing systems properly. Also, one mistake in setting up and the business could quickly become insolvent, bankrupt or liquidated. This is why MLM companies are often considered a safer option for generating extra income in business.

Building your network

When it comes to joining an MLM organisation it's all about growing off the back of an existing business. You buy into an existing system and stem from it. Using the MLM company's product you can build your own fortune by simply building your own network.

There are three key things you need to know in order to build your network successfully.

1. **To be successful you must overcome your fear of being rejected**.

   Put yourself out there. Remember, the wider your network is the better. Self-confidence is crucial. If you don't believe in the product you are selling then why should anyone else? (Look back at the points raised in chapter 2 about "the SW attitude". You will need to apply some of these principles for this type of business.)

2. **Learn how to work with other sales reps.**

   Working in teams with other sales reps and learning how they operate will help build your network. Having that natural flair to inspire others to join is great. But if you don't have it, you could either spend days improving on your sales pitch, or get another sales rep to do your pitching for you. They may be much better at it, so you can still make sales without worrying about being a good salesperson.

3. **You will be required to pull your weight**.

It would be wrong of me to give the impression that by joining an MLM all your dreams will be instantly fulfilled. Before you can even think about earning £70,000 residual income you must first work hard building your network. It normally requires you to dedicate a few months to constant networking. Only after this period will you be able to earn a decent commission from your down line.

Advantages and disadvantages

Not everyone is cut out for joining an MLM organisation. Before you choose to sign up to anything please have a look through the short summary of pros and cons.

Advantages

- Usually start-up **costs are low.**
- Many of the highest-quality **products** are manufactured by MLM companies.
- You can work it **part time** if you choose, which allows you to work a job fulltime and work your MLM business in your spare time.
- You can **work from your home**.
- Your business **expenses will be deductible** from your income tax.
- You will **be your own boss.**
- You **choose which hours** you want to work.
- You may develop a small **extra income** or possibly even a very large income, allowing you to quit your job, or have a great retirement.
- Your income will be a **"residual" income**, which will come to you month after month, year after year.
- You will have **time freedom**.
- You will meet many **like-minded people**.

Disadvantages

- At first you could work very, **very hard** without

making any money!

- The ease of start-up can cause people to get into several companies, with the mistaken belief that they can easily develop several income streams. This causes a **lack of focus** and makes the person far more likely to fail.
- **The products** could be overpriced and it may be difficult to determine whether they are any better than you could purchase at a discount store.
- There are a lot **of very inaccurate "get-rich quick" claims** out there. When success doesn't come quickly, a person may be more likely to quit and join something else.
- It can be very hard to distinguish a legitimate company or opportunity from **a scam.**
- Ideally, MLM is based on everyone doing a little bit. In reality, most **people don't do their part**, making it necessary for the few workers to work much harder to find any amount of success!
- The **failure rate** is actually higher than the success rate. It only works if you and your team work.
- As in any business, to succeed with MLM takes a lot of **dedication**.
- You must be the one to decide to work it, or invest your money into advertising. It takes true **self-discipline**!

FRANCHISE

Another business structure you may want to consider is to own a franchise. A franchise is the right granted to an individual or group to market a company's goods or services within a certain location. Subway, Pizza Hut, and possibly the most famous of all, McDonalds are all international franchises.

There are many different types of franchise nowadays. Not all franchises need to be multinational restaurant chains. You can own a franchise of a vending machine for as little as £300. Then you can set this up at any location you wish.

How it helps you

Franchising began back in the 1850's when Isaac Singer invented the sewing machine. In order to distribute his machines outside of his geographical area, and also provide training to customers, Singer began selling licenses to entrepreneurs in different parts of the country.

Today, the franchising business structure is helping thousands of individuals be their own boss and own their own business.

Franchising allows entrepreneurs to be in business for themselves, but not by themselves. By owning a franchise you have more chance to be successful than by setting up on your own. Similar to joining an MLM organisation, a franchise gives you a proven business formula and systems. The products, services and business operations have already been established.

As a student you may not have time to spend creating a product then creating a system to get it to market and promote it. This saves you years of time trying to build a brand. In the long run franchising will also save money and energy trying to build up your own business from scratch. Therefore you will be working smarter and not harder.

How it works

If you were to purchase a franchise you would be known as a franchis*ee*. Franchis*ees* are the individuals or groups that buy a franchise from the franch*iser*. If I own a pizza shop I am the franchis*er.* If you decided to buy a franchise of my pizza shop from me and set it up on your university campus you would then be the franchis*ee* of the pizza shop.

Although you now own that particular restaurant on campus you must still abide by the rules and regulation I set as the franchi*ser*. In most agreements the franchisers may also request royalty fees to be paid to them from the money the franchisee makes selling at their location.

Use of Brand

One of other major reasons entrepreneurs find buying franchises so worthwhile is because you get to use the corporate image. A franchise that has a strong following means you stand to earn more profit by using their corporate image and brand awareness. This also helps when trying to gain consumer trust.

You can probably testify yourself that as a consumer you're always more confortable purchasing items from familiar names that you trust. The popularity of the brand is normally a key factor in the franchisee success. Franchisers know this, and usually reflect it in the price they sell the franchise for.

Support from the franchiser

The success of every franchising organisation relies on the standardisation of their outlets. The quality of chicken at a Nandos restaurant in London must be the same as the chicken from the Manchester outlet. You may also notice that the atmosphere, decoration and furniture of every outlet are the same. To get such high levels of standardisation the franchiser must provide extensive training and support to the franchise owner.

Most franchisers help their franchisees develop a marketing plan, with some parts being procedures to guarantee uniformity throughout all the branches and others being suited to the needs of the individual franchisee. The franchiser may also offer advice on developing a campaign for your local area.

So as a franchisee you can rest in the knowledge that you will also have constant support from the head office.

A much-quoted catchphrase in the franchising sector is "you're on your own, but not alone." The company already knows how they want things run, it's part of their business model. Therefore you have less to focus on and more time to get down to work.

Do your research

If you want to buy a franchise I suggest your first move should be to research it. There are over 1,500 franchise opportunities in the UK alone. All are different and operate in different ways. Find one that you can work with. To predict the potential of your franchise, consider the number already operating under the same name, the number that have failed and the length of time the franchiser and its franchisees have been in operation.

Remember, you don't want to fall into the trap and work in the franchise, but you want to own the franchise. This may mean once you set up your outlet finding people to work in it to run it for you. This is costly but in the long run you may find it a very worthwhile investment. I suggest you consult a franchise attorney before diving into any abrupt agreement.

<u>Advantages and disadvantages</u>

In summary here is a list of some of the advantages and more, plus the downside to franchising.

Advantages

- There is a **lower risk of failure** than for an independent business because you are offering a service or product that already sells successfully.
- The franchiser will offer **training** and the benefit of its experience, offering **advice** every step of the way.
- You will also be offered continuous **management assistance** with accounting, personnel, facilities and so on.
- Franchisers develop, refine and set in place

operational standards that help ensure a consistent level of quality.
- Regional and **national marketing** is prepared and disseminated by the franchiser through experienced advertising businesses.
- **Lower-cost goods** and supplies will be available because of the superior purchasing power of your franchiser.

Disadvantages
- The **initial start-up cost**, which typically can range from a few thousand pounds for a franchise based at home, to several hundred thousand pounds for a franchise with its own premises.
- You pay franchiser **royalties -** usually under ten per cent of your franchise's gross income.
- Your figures and operation standards will be **regularly scrutinised** by your franchiser.
- If you have a better idea for doing something, conformity to operational standards may become restrictive.
- There is always the danger that your **franchiser is weak**, inexperienced or under-financed. It is not unknown for franchisers to fail.
- You will be **under contract** to run your business for a specified number of years, so you won't be able to quit without a penalty and you would lose the money you paid up front.

E-COMMERCE

E-commerce is the buying and selling of goods and services on the Internet. It's often referred to as a newer term, e-business. For online retail selling, the term e-tailing is sometimes used.

Use of being online

One of the greatest things about the internet is that it is operating 24/7. When you're sleeping the business is still selling. It's not surprising that over the past decade more and more entrepreneurs have decided to set up online stores.

The latest generation of young entrepreneurs are growing up with the internet. Everything you need for business has become more readily available than it was 20 years ago. Thanks to the ease of access when it comes to starting a business online, many bright entrepreneurs have emerged whilst still in their teens. Social networks have also opened the doors for anyone to engage in free marketing of their business on the web.

The internet is also a more common place to see teens who have taught themselves code and are able to create innovative web apps due to the freedom they possess. Something may start out as hobby or after-school project but you can turn it into a real business for yourself.

There are endless opportunities to make money online. Although websites are easy to start there is a lot of detail that must be considered to get online selling right. Three crucial aspects must be in place regardless of what you plan to sell or do online. These are the WEBSITE, THE TRAFFIC and THE CONVERSION which are all explained in detail below.

<u>Website</u>

The first key consideration should be the actual site.

Audience and structure

Your actual site must be done to a required standard that suits your needs. Before you start building it make sure you define your audience. This is fundamental, but many people forget it! What audience do you want to reach? Is your website for business partners, potential investors, children or institutional bodies? The target audience determines what content you present.

With regards to your content most of your visitors won't know the subject as well as you do, and have little time to spend reading! So keep it simple and short. Avoid jargon, keep it easy to read and easy to navigate. Visitors should ideally find information in 2-3 clicks maximum.

Looks are everything

If it's a professional company they should have a professional site. A good design reflects well on your organisation or project. Do not go over the top with graphic content. Multimedia can make your content more attractive but only if it supports your message, otherwise leave it out. White space has proven to be important in communications. Also large images may slow the page from loading.

Along with looks is the name of the site. Before people visit your site they will subconsciously judge its worth by its domain name. Be careful when deciding this. For example sites with the letter "x" in them are quickly associated with the porn industry so refrain from using that too much. Also make it easy to remember. Today people remember website names as we used to remember phone numbers. So make sure that your domain name is clear and catchy.

Update your content regularly

Sites with regularly changing content attract more visitors. Archive what's out-of-date, and replace it with new content. Also ensure that you don't have broken links. If a visitor is looking for something in particular have a 'search engine' box on the front page.

The regular visitors will appreciate the constant updating of the site. They are the most valuable visitors so it would be good to make them feel a part of it. Give your site an interactive feel. Allow visitors to interact with the content author or producer. Host a discussion forum or start a blog. It will influence whether your visitors look at your site occasionally or regularly.

Traffic

Once you have created your website content, you have to attract your audience to it.

Submit your site to search engines

Make sure you have keywords in your content. Search engines pick these up. The words should mirror what users would type to find your pages (most search services index each word in an html file). Use short, accurate descriptions to identify your site.

Ask for reciprocal links

You can gain visibility on search engines as well as attracting more visitors by having other sites link to yours. For example, you can publish links to your associating websites or websites of friends and ask them to return the favour.

Submit your links to directories. Search for the major research factors in your field such as well-reputed web portals, and have your website added to their link section or directory.

Issue news releases and submit to press wires

Be media-friendly. Send news releases about your events and achievements to print and web periodicals. This may attract journalists to look at your project and publicise it. Offer content for others to use in their newsletters and sites.

You can increase your visibility when you write articles in your area of expertise and supply them to editors for their newsletters. Just ask that they include a link to your website and a one-line description of what you offer.

Promote online and offline email

Though it takes a lot of time, consider publishing a

monthly e-mail newsletter. This is a good way to bring users to your website. But remember - it is important not to spam, so do not send e-mails without permission to people who do not want them.

Promote your website everywhere the best you can. You can do this at conferences, in web forums and in your email signature. Include your web address on business cards and promotional materials. Ensure that all reprints of cards, stationery and marketing materials contain your web address.

Conversion

Many websites concentrate solely on increasing the number of visitors they have. Conversion is all about how you transfer all that traffic coming to your site into cash. Without a good conversion rate, nothing about your online business is profitable.

Offer Different Payment Options

It might sound obvious, but you should offer the user a reasonable selection of methods of payment. Not everybody has a credit card, and those that do don't always want to use them. You don't have to accept cheques, but when deciding on payment methods consider alternatives to the usual methods. Make the users feel at ease and give them what they want.

Track everything

Using things like Google analytics keeps a record of activity to and from your site. Use this to your advantage. Find out where most of your visitors are coming from, what countries are people buying from, what sites are not really useful in directing people to yours and look to improve.

Most important of course, when looking at the conversion rate, is the volume of sales. Some people only look at that number. But other numbers can tell you about how useful your site is throughout the shopping process.

The percentage of repeat visitors tells you something about whether you are engaging visitors early in the purchasing process and bringing them back for the sale. A high bounce rate indicates pages that are failing to deliver on their promises. Add to cart rates, cart abandonment rates, login vs. registration vs. abandonment rates, product removal (from cart) rates - all of these will identify areas of your checkout and purchase process that are underperforming or improving.

Be clear on pricing strategy

Pricing is tricky for almost every industry. Price yourself too high and you'll lose out to cheaper competitors. Price yourself too low and you'll end up appearing cheap. Price some products high and others low and you'll look like you're pushing some brands over others.

It's important to be clear with your pricing - if you're aiming to be the cheapest then go all out and be the cheapest. Offer price comparisons or price matching. If you're going for higher prices and selling quality of service, don't shout about your expensive prices. Let your advertising be geared towards the quality of what your customers are paying for.

This also applies to shipping. Delivery costs are almost always an additional expense incurred during the checkout process. If you add delivery costs during the checkout process, then exactly when you don't want people reconsidering their purchase, you're giving them a reason to. Make delivery free or flat rate and add it from the start of the shopping process. There's no harm in reducing delivery cost - and telling the customer you've done so - during the checkout process.

Once you have mastered how to do the website, traffic and conversion the way it should be done, you can truly call yourself a student entrepreneur and not just someone that has a website.

Advantages and disadvantages

As with everything there are always pros and cons.

Advantages

- **Lower start-up costs**, websites can be set up for free nowadays.
- An internet business gives you a **global web presence** so you can sell and attract customers from different markets all over the world.
- Your business generates passive income and does so even after working hours. This is very profitable because sales are costly to conduct **24/7**.
- The web presence allows you to give customers a **quicker response**. You can also be notified more quickly if there are any problems with your site or product.
- When you are a student entrepreneur, not everyone takes you seriously. Being an online business allows you to present a **professional front**. Nobody needs to know that your huge fantastic organisation is actually run by one individual.
- Setting up online means you can take your business with you all the time. You have the luxury to **work from home** or in your college library.

Disadvantages

- You can't physically see customers so it's **harder to build relationships** with them.
- The constant need to **maintain sites** can be tiring. If you don't have a website manager you will need to be doing the regular updates yourself.
- Because of the nature of the internet there will always be a **lack of customer trust**. With so many dodgy, unsafe sites on the web, only the well-known reputable sites make millions.

JOINT VENTURES

Some of you reading this may already be up and running in your business. Regardless of how you set up your work, it's not too late to structure it smart. You can still achieve your ambitious sales targets without overworking yourself and pulling away from your studies. Possibly one of the most successful strategies to do so for your business is to transform your company structure into a joint venture.

A joint venture is an organisation in which two or more individuals or companies join together in a partnership. These two business or groups will then combine their resources in the hopes of accomplishing a specific, profitable goal. For example, two oil companies might form a joint venture to drill a new well. Many entrepreneurs base their whole company on the relationships with others. Sometime it can cost you absolutely nothing to leverage your business profit and even quadruple your sales without much time or effort on your part. This is the power of knowing how to form joint ventures. While you are studying you will not have the time or resources to do everything but you can still make a huge fortune by making the right partnerships.

McDonalds and Disney

These are two companies not in direct competition with each other but who have the same target market. They have both tapped into the billions of pounds in advertising capital already invested by the other partner without spending a fraction of that to do so.

Have you ever noticed how McDonalds always have figurines of Disney characters in their happy meals? The toy also changes month by month, keeping up with the most recent Disney film release.

This is one part of their strategic joint venture. Every time a child carries around their happy meal toy its free advertising for the new movie. The more the child plays with the toy the more he or she builds up a strong desire to watch the film. So parents will take their children to the movies. Before you know it Disney's latest animated film becomes a box office hit thanks to their ability to tap into McDonalds' customer base.

However, it doesn't end there. Have you ever noticed that on the back of your cinema ticket you are usually offered a coupon voucher from - guess who... McDonalds! Also, have you ever wondered why every time you walk out of the cinema there is usually a McDonalds restaurant within five minutes? This is the second part of their joint venture. Customers at the cinema reason with themselves to quickly pop into McDonalds since they have a coupon voucher. Soon enough, McDonalds' tills are ringing because they have tapped into Disney's customer base.

The result is a significant increase in both businesses. It has proven to be one of the most successful examples of using joint ventures because the relationship has lasted for several decades.

How I did it

Whilst running the football coaching academy we reached a point where the sales were constant for a long time.

I was really hungry to see the rapid growth of the business. However, I didn't have time to chase customers because I still had midterms and final exams to focus on. I sat down with my team of managers and we discussed the issues and asked ourselves 3 key questions:

- **Who are our best customers? (The answer was an obvious one –Kids.)**
- **Who else is involved in the decision making process? (Parents)**
- **Who else shares our market, or has captured our market, doesn't compete with our product but in fact can complement our product? (Schools !!!)**

This was another eureka moment that helped structure my business around my studies. I instantly printed a flyer advertising free coaching sessions for schools. I was able to get in contact with several schools and agree a date and time to pop in and run a one-off taster sessions for their student sports day. This was great for the school because they looked like they were reaching their extra curriculum targets without spending a penny of their budget. It was also great for me because I was able to give the students a taster of how fun our weekend coaching session was.

It wasn't very long after that that I had many of those school children enquiring about how to join the coaching academy and signing up for more regular sessions. I didn't need to spend any time or money worrying about fishing for new clients. I knew as long as I was engaged in this joint venture with schools my sales would continue to grow rapidly. And they did.

The three key questions above may be something that you will need to ask yourself in order to identify your best potential joint venture partners. A joint venture does not need to be with obvious companies that are in the same industry. I've heard of a jewellery store and bookstores that have used this structure successfully. For every £30 spent on books customers were entered into a competition to win a diamond. However, they had to visit the jewellery store to find out whether they had won.

I have even heard of successful joint ventures with hairdressers and accountants. Sweets shops and car dealerships, supermarkets and rock concerts… the list is endless. Once again it requires thinking outside the box and finding ways of adding value to your partner's clients in order for them to become your clients.

The 8 Steps for a successful Joint Venture

1. **Identify your target market** – who are your customers?

2. **Identify other interests** your target market might have –commercially, socially, spiritually, sporting, recreation, leisure. What else do they do and where else do they spend their money?

3. **Identify other businesses that have already captured the market you're targeting.**

4. **Create a compelling and irresistible offer** that will be enticing and exciting enough to generate enough interest in the prospective partner that will **get them to sit down with you**. Don't go for everything all at once; start with a meeting, nothing more.

5. **Make it Win–Win.** Work out an arrangement that will be mutually beneficial to everyone involved. This is called a win-win and it is crucial you know how to position your prospective partner's potential win out of the relationship.

6. **Agree on an action plan** on each side. Keep them to a minimum and keep them very simple. Simple gets done.

7. **Set a deadline** to get it implemented. It should be no longer than two weeks, otherwise you have over an 80% chance that the joint venture partner deal will fall over.

8. **Get an endorsement** from the joint venture partner if possible. Make them a customer by offering free products or services and take the time to make sure they "love" what you do, or at the least "like" it.

Build Rapport

Relationships are very important to the success of your joint venture. No-one likes to feel like they are just being used and they shouldn't. Do not be shy about taking an interest in your partners' private needs. After you've done business together offer to meet up with them regularly to discuss long-term ventures. At these meetings it would be a good idea to take some notes and **listen carefully**.

Regular meetings are also good for you to decide whether these partners are still valuable to you.

If you do feel they are right for you, you will want to secure the partnership. Help them see the benefits it could bring. Get them talking about their business and the challenges they have, and try to take them to a point of admitting they would like to increase their customer base and make more money. Here are 11 questions you can ask:

"How long have you been in business?"
"How many offices do you have?"
"Are you busy throughout the whole year? When are your quiet periods?"
"What are your top two challenges in your business?"
"How do you win new business?"
"How do you plan on growing your business in the next few years?"
"How often do you keep in contact with your customers?"
"When was the last time you gave your clients some sort of gift?"

"Do you think giving them a gift creates a better relationship between you and them?"
"How do you keep in contact – phone, email, mail?" (They will usually say mail)
"So, that must cost you a bit of money? Do you use a database? How many people do you have on your database? Do you mail to all of them?"

Advantages and disadvantages

Because of their many benefits, joint ventures are very common. However, there are also a number of drawbacks.

Advantages

- Joint ventures allow different parties to bring **different skills** to the table. Many companies enter into joint partnerships to gain access to new technology, capital and skills, as well as critical business knowledge.
- Some countries will only allow foreign companies to enter local markets by making joint ventures with local businesses. This allows the country to provide new products and services to its citizens and for the foreign companies to **reach new markets**.
- As companies are combining their resources in a joint venture, they also **share risk**. This makes joint ventures a wise move for particularly risky transactions, allowing companies to essentially hedge their bets.

Disadvantages

- If the majority of your sales rely on the input of your joint venture partner then there could be a danger of **over-dependency on your partner.**
- Joint ventures means that **decision making takes far longer** than in other instances, as each issue must be negotiated until all parties are in agreement.
- The flip side to sharing risks is that **rewards must**

also be divided. This presents a severe downside to forming joint ventures for companies that believe they can conduct a successful transaction on their own.

- Each company has its own culture, philosophy and management style. Unless all parties in a joint venture agree there could be **potential for disagreements**.

CHAPTER 7

FUNDING AND RESOURCING

When starting your company whilst still very young, a big concern is how seriously people will take you as a young entrepreneur. It is hard enough when trying to work with suppliers and partners. How about when trying to get funding? It gets a lot easier as you grow and build evidence that your business is making money and your model is working, but it can often take a lot of attempts to get there. In this chapter I will be showing you different ways you can fund your projects and how to get off to the best start without a huge budget.

BE RESOURCEFUL, BE RELENTLESS

What resourceful actually means

I recently looked in the dictionary for the definition of the word 'resourceful' and it gives the meaning as "ingenious, capable, and full of initiative, especially in dealing with difficult situations."

I don't think any word can describe a student entrepreneur better. Too many people use lack of money as an excuse for not starting their business. The reason these people are not entrepreneurs is because they are not resourceful or relentless. It's the difference between being resourceful and passively waiting for resources like money to fall into your lap.

Financing your venture does not need to be a major problem when you learn how to be resourceful.

Friends and family

What separates those who achieve from those who do not is in direct proportion to their ability to ask for help. One of the benefits of having friends is that you can pull in favours. There have been many times that I have needed someone to help organise an event or do admin work while I'm running around. I always call on a trustworthy friend or family member. These simple tasks can be done by anyone. The more favours I call in, the more money it saves me in the long run.

If it is a job that they have done exceptionally well and it really does deserve payment then offer to pay them at a later date when you have better cash flow. Integrity is key; never make a promise about money to someone if you will not keep it. If you fail to keep your word, the next time you need a favour you may realise you have less friends than before.

There will be many occasions when you have poor cash flow or are on a tight budget; this is where the power of networking and building strong relationships can help, especially within your own industry. Networking is not about who has the most friends, it's about whose friends are most valuable.

As a football coach I often liaised with football scouts, youth club managers, fitness and health advisors. These friendships were not really useful when I needed someone to design a poster for free or someone to film and edit a promo video for the academy. This is why I also networked with people that were outside of my industry, such as designers and even film directors. They may not be directly linked to the sports industry but proved the most useful when I needed a favour done.

People will always be your biggest asset. Even if people can't do the work for you, they may still be able to help by letting you use their tools, equipment and contacts to get the job done. If you don't ask you won't know.

Assess what is available to you

This day and age, there are endless opportunities to get hold of anything you want. I had a friend who was a songwriter. He could not afford to pay a big producer for a beat to his songs so he went on YouTube and found other producers that were giving out instrumental beats for free. This is just one example of how easy it is to get the same quality without paying a high price.

The power of the internet means that you can learn how to do practically anything you want online. It means you can simply teach yourself how to make I-phone apps and sell them. You may not have a publishing contract but you can learn how to write and self-publish your own book. You can even learn how to play guitar without paying for a tutor.

Rather than quitting or changing your goal, be relentless and keep finding ways to get what you want. A next best alternative will always come to mind. In the last section of this book there is a comprehensive list of resources that are available and can help you get well on your way.

ACCESS TO FUNDING

Venture capital

Venture capital or VC refers to people or organisations that regularly invest in high risk start up business projects. VCs are very attractive for new companies with a limited operating history, that are too small to raise capital in the public markets and have not reached the point where they are able to secure a bank loan or complete a debt offering.

Venture capital investors are only interested in companies with high growth prospects, which are managed by experienced and ambitious teams who are capable of turning their business plan into reality. They invest in exchange for an equity stake in the business. Although they can provide you with a large sum of money for a good business idea, they will take a considerably huge stake of your business. Personally I wouldn't advise this as the best route to funding. Before you approach a VC, always try to use one of the other sources of funding below.

Grants

Grants are free pots of money that you never need to pay back and they are available almost everywhere. You could get a grant through central government and the European Union, or your local authority. Some universities also offer grants to small businesses. It pays to do your research into this. Ask around. The application process may be long at times but for free money it's worth it.

Grants and other funding are often targeted at specific types of spending. You should have a clear idea of what you are investing money into. Grants are also offered to support deprived rural or urban areas. If you can prove your business helps the community, and in what way, you stand a good chance of being funded.

Competitions

Another avenue for free money is the reward offered in various competitions. Things like business plan competitions are becoming very popular nowadays. You simply submit your business concept and the most creative bid will win the money. Business is big money and in some competitions you can stand to win around £50,000. I saw a competition recently which was awarding £175,000 free to the best idea.

Another benefit of competitions is that in most cases they don't just give you money but also help with starting up and provide access to other resources like lawyers and mentorship. Business competitions are everywhere; check your local papers, and online.

The only negative part about the whole competition process is that there are many other businesses all going out to win. You must make sure your idea is good enough to stand against other applicants.

Government schemes

Laws are always changing with regards to where the government is investing tax payers' money. Keep an eye out for government schemes that encourage entrepreneurship. They usually have loads of money to give away or lend to small business to grow. Things such as the enterprise finance guarantee (EFG) are basically loans that you can get from your bank without having to put your house on the line as collateral. Therefore it's quite a low risk loan.

However, the bank's risk is usually covered by government. Banks hate loaning money to small businesses so this initiative was designed to encourage more lending. There is an interest rate on the loan and it usually varies. Once again do research into which is best for you.

TOP 10 REASONS WHY FUNDING BIDS GET REJECTED

To increase your chances for success, it is useful to know how funders think about the bids they receive and what criteria they deploy. I did some research into this and below is a typical list of reasons that funders gave for why they refused applications in the past.

1. **"The organisation does not meet our priorities"** - research thoroughly before applying
2. **"The organisation is not located in our geographical area of funding"** – get the guidelines before applying
3. **"The proposal does not follow our prescribed format"** - read the application information carefully and follow it in detail
4. **"The proposal is poorly written or difficult to understand"** – ask experienced people to critique

your application before you submit it

5. **"The proposed budget/grant request is not within our funding range"**- look at the average size of grants given by the funder
6. **"We don't know these people, are they credible?"** – try to set up an interview before submitting your proposal and ask board members and other funded organisations to help establish a relationship or give you credibility
7. **"The proposal doesn't seem urgent. I'm not sure it'll have an impact"** – study the priorities and get a skilled writer to do this section so it 'grabs' the funder. Sound urgent, but not in crisis
8. **"The objectives and plan of the action of the project greatly exceed the budget and timelines for the implementation"** – be realistic about programmes of activities and budgets - only promise what can really be delivered for the amount you request
9. **"We've had too many applicants and have already allocated all the money for this grant cycle"** – don't take this personally. It is a fact of life. Try the next grant cycle. Next time, submit at least a month before the deadline to give ample opportunity for your proposal to be reviewed
10. **"There is not enough evidence that the project will become self-sufficient and sustain itself after the grant is completed"** – add a section to the proposal on your exit plan and develop a long term strategy to show how you'll manage on your own

MONEY MANAGEMENT

Maximise your student discount

One major advantage of being a student entrepreneur is that your student status usually gets you things for discount prices. Going to the movies, riding the bus, or even ordering pizza might cost less if you show your student I.D. Check travel fares for student discounts on bus and other commercial transit services as well as student discounts when you need to travel by air.

Budget

Gather your available cash including gift money. Allocate money from student loans, summer job savings and money from your parents into your venture. You may want to designate money for certain uses. Rather than going shopping with your bank card, why not withdraw the exact amount of cash you need and shop on that. This stops you from buying unnecessary things that you fancied when you saw them in shop windows.

As you save to finance your big idea you are less tempted to blow that extra bit of money you have. Budgeting also helps you keep a record of your spending; once you realise how much impulse buying and other indulgences cost you, it will be easier to tell yourself "NO!"

Budget for a month at a time but set aside some time to review your finances each week. A budget is like a money diet. Just because you bust it today, doesn't mean you can't start it again tomorrow. If you go over budget this week, next week commit to staying under budget.

Put your roommate in your budgeting plan. If you can, contact your roommate before the semester starts and decide how you'll divide expenses like groceries and phone hook-up charges.

Be cautious

Don't give anyone your Social Security, credit card, or bank account numbers unless you know why they need them. Never give a pin number to anyone! Don't leave bill payment envelopes at your mailbox, especially if you live in student halls. Drop them in a secured draw.

Being safe with your finances seems quite obvious but students are the worst when it comes to being cautious. Make sure you review credit card statements, bank statements, phone bills, etc. for unauthorised use.

Keep a calendar of dates

As you keep applying for financial aid, make sure you keep track of the important deadline dates. Missing an application deadline is the most common mistake students make when applying for scholarships, grants or bursaries.

Bill payment dates are clearly important or they can end up charging you the extra late payment fee. You can make bill paying easier by filing your bills by due date. Upcoming school expenses such as books and tuition fees should also be noted. Also write down upcoming activities where you'll need cash such as movies, dances, parties, etc.

Buy books when you need them.

Compare online prices with those at campus bookstores. Buy used books when you can. Check noticeboards and school newspapers as well as used bookstores and online used booksellers.

CHAPTER 8

SALES AND MARKETING

Sales and marketing are an art form. If you cannot learn to sell or market your product or service, it is going to be very difficult to get anywhere with your venture.

THE SALES PROCESS

Selling has a bad reputation because so many people who are in sales are so hopeless or sleazy. However, when you meet a good and proper salesperson you will not even be aware you've just been sold something. Instead you'll come away with the warm feeling that you have just made a brilliant decision to buy something. This is how marketing is supposed to be done.

When conducting closing sales there is a four stage process that you want the buyer to go through.

Find suspects
You first want to find the right people or organisation that can be potential buyers. Consider who the product is targeted for. Also consider if the user is also the intended buyer. Usually with products targeted at children, the sales person doesn't pitch to the child themselves but to the parents because they will make the buying decision.

Also do lots of market research to find your suspects. Look at area, demographic and other markets where there could be demand for the product or service you have to offer. Read and listen to the media to find out who is talking about your product. Where there is interest there is also a potential sale.

1. Make them prospects
Once you have found the group of people that share an interest in your product or service, the next stage is to

discern who the real prospects are. These are the ones that actually have the ability to purchase the product and not just be interested in it. Everyone wants to drive a Porsche but not everyone can afford it. Therefore only focus your attention and energy on those that are actually prospects. These are the ones that you present your offer to.

2. Make them customers

Once you have found your prospects and they have accepted your offer they are now your customers. They have bought what you're selling; you have closed the deal and reached your goal. However, your job is not done yet. Your business will benefit from making them regular customers and you must find ways to keep them with you should they want to purchase again.

3. Turn them into evangelists

After a few repeat sales it's safe to say you have a nice base of regular customers. You no longer need to convince them that your product is worth buying. Your goal now is to turn these customers into raving fanatics. You want them to love your product so much that they can't help but tell their friends about it. You will make more money in the long run from having evangelists rather than just customers.

GETTING THE CLOSE

A crucial stage in the whole sales process is actually getting the close. This is the turning point when a prospect becomes a customer. If your product doesn't sell itself people generally won't buy it, unless they are desperate or they like you. Surveys show that people generally buy products they don't even like simply because the sales person was nice. This is why your approach to the close must be done properly.

You do not want to come across as a bully or as a suck-up who charms your way into people's wallets. Take a genuine interest in what the customer wants and be passionate about what you're selling.

Below is a proven model of how to close the sale. I suggest you follow each step until you have completed the close and the whole negotiation is a 100% done deal. I will run you through each step to getting the vital job done.

(5% complete) Send a letter – once you have highlighted your prospect, find the intended buyer's contact details and send them a personalised letter inviting them to try your product (not buy! That will come at a later stage). Include brochures, flyers or any piece of information they can have to hand that tells them enough about your business. E-mails can also work but most people will quickly delete junk mail online.

(10% complete) Phone them up – the chances are you probably won't hear from them straight away. You don't even know if the intended recipient got your letter. It may not have even got past the secretary. This is why you wait for three days then give them a follow up call to ask if they have seen the letter. If you wait longer they may have forgotten about the letter if they did read it, if you do it before three days it could be too soon. Over the phone you have an opportunity to explain the contents of the letter further and build a rapport with the prospect.

(30% complete) Determine if they are a real prospect – as you are getting to know your prospect, be a good listener. You might find out some information that will give you a clearer idea if this is a lead worth pursuing or not. For example, if you're setting up a summer camp but find out that your prospect will be overseas for the summer, this is not a lead worth chasing.

(45% complete) Do a demo – whenever the opportunity arises, it will be good to give the prospect a demo. People are more convinced by what they experience rather than what you tell them.

(55% complete) Give a quote – present the prospect with a clear and fair quote. It's usually a good idea to start high then let them bargain you down to a lower price that you are comfortable with.

(70% complete) Deal with competitive issues –there may be competitors in your field that can match your quote or even beat it. At this point you throw in something extra that won't cost you extra. Or you can highlight your unique selling point. This is something competitors cannot match.

(90% complete) Get an order – collect details for an order. Make this quick and easy for the buyer. You are 90% on your way to a close. You do not want the buyer to be frustrated by loads of paper work and change their mind.

(95% complete) Fulfil the order – fulfil the order and keep to your promise. Make sure you keep to the quality standard you both agreed on. Make sure the item or service is delivered on time. If the buyer is not happy with what they got they can still return it and walk away from the deal at this stage.

(100% complete) Get paid – if the buyer is satisfied then you have got the job done. You have successfully closed the deal. Take your money and keep in touch with the customer so he or she becomes a regular.

24 HABITS OF EFFECTIVE SALES PEOPLE

An excellent sales person will learn and master each of these habits. To be effective you should be good at:

1. Communicating the message that it's sound business to trust you
2. Asking the right questions
3. Taking the lead
4. Engaging the prospect
5. Finding key requirements
6. Converting the leads that "fall into your lap"
7. Knowing how to make your product or service fit somewhere else
8. Pretending you're a consultant (because you are!)
9. Asking for the next appointment whilst you are on your first visit
10. Taking notes
11. Creating a plan with each new prospect
12. Asking for referrals
13. Showing enthusiasm
14. Giving yourself appropriate credit
15. Telling the truth (it's easier to remember!)
16. Selling yourself
17. Starting early
18. Reading industry publications
19. Giving speeches to businesses and local groups
20. Passing along the opportunity when appropriate
21. Taking responsibility for presentations that go wrong
22. Being honest with yourself about the nature of the firm you work with
23. Telling everyone you meet who you are and what you sell
24. Keeping your sense of humour!

MARKETING TOOLS EVERY START UP SHOULD USE

When you start your venture you will find that marketing is on-going. I know many companies that spend most of their revenue just on advertising. The simplest way to be cost effective in marketing is to have a product that speaks for itself. The old saying of "build a product people want to talk about" still holds today.

Word of mouth is the most effective form of marketing. You can save a whole load of money by having a product or service people really love, and that might be all the marketing you need. In a recent survey about influential marketing, 14% of participants said they trusted adverts, whereas the remaining 86% preferred to trust other people's recommendations.

However, even with a product people love, you'll need to sustain the interest and there's no harm in generating more of a buzz. Here are several tools for marketing your venture on a very low budget.

Build up your company and personal profile

Many of the most talked-about start-up ventures are run by people who are high profile. These are people who work very hard to build their own personal profiles and brands. They're promoting themselves as a means of promoting their companies. Focus on building trust, reputation and thought leadership, even at a small scale, and you'll see results.

Start a company blog

There's really no reason you shouldn't have a blog. Everyone is blogging nowadays, but it remains an effective way to build interest. Company blogs are interesting because they don't just represent the voice of a single person; they represent the voice of a company. This is certainly different from a personal blog. Blogs also help people find you online. The more your name is on the internet the higher you will appear in search rankings.

Use viral videos

A viral video is a video that people pass around to their friend on the internet. "Charlie bit my finger" and other incredible, shocking or comical clips on YouTube are great examples. This approach is more of a "shot in the dark" compared to having a blog. Nevertheless, it's worth trying. Humour tends to works best.

Social media

Twitter, Facebook, LinkedIn, YouTube and other popular social networking websites are the lifesavers of marketing. The power of social media has allowed anyone to start up a marketing campaign for free. One of the really good things about social media is that it allows you to track your brand. You can easily find out what people are saying about you and get feedback from your customers.

Social media is also a lot less formal so it is often considered more welcoming to approach people on these platforms, as opposed to sticking posters in their face.

MARKETING STRATEGY

What is a marketing strategy?

Having a clear marketing strategy will make your venture more profitable. Entrepreneurs that employ a marketing strategy tend to focus on their customers and markets. Writing a marketing plan is different from having a business plan. In your marketing strategy you will need to define objectives and describe the way you're going to satisfy customers in your chosen markets. It helps to have a marketing plan in place as your funders or investors will often ask to see it before showing interest in your venture.

The key in marketing strategy is to understand and match the capabilities of your firm to the opportunities available in the market. You will therefore need to do lots of research and gather information on different areas such as:

Your Market: data about the size and growth rate of the market, who your potential customers are, what they buy, when they buy, from whom and through whom do they buy, etc.

Your Competitive Environment: data on who are your direct competitors, what are your competitors up to, their products, prices, etc. It also helps to identify indirect or potential competitors who may take you by surprise.

Your Internal Operation: data within your business will help to assess the strengths and weaknesses of your product/service and its core capabilities. What resources do you have available, what have you not yet tried.

Once you have gathered all this information you will have a good basis to start planning your venture's marketing strategy.

Marketing objectives

Just because you're in business it doesn't necessarily mean your aim is to make the most profit. There may be other objectives you would want to pursue such as gaining more market share, sales or market share growth, market entry, increased awareness, etc.

To do so you may need to forfeit profit in the short run, however it will position you in a better standing in the market in the long run. Amazon is the world's number 1 when it comes to online book selling. However, when the company first started they didn't take in any profit for 11 years. All the money they were making was reinvested in the company for over a decade. Because of this they now stand in a solid position in their market. Whatever you decide your business objective to be, remember your marketing objective should address it.

Focus on the 4 Ps. The **products**, **price**, **place** (distribution) and **promotion** that you are using as 'marketing tools' to deliver benefits to your customers, beat competitors and achieve your objective.

Also consider targeting segments. Having a niche or some kind of specific customer groups or segments you are targeting is often more beneficial, rather than marketing to everyone because you assume that will get you more sales.

Your objectives will influence how you implement your marketing. This includes your action plans, budgets, timescales and resources. The best marketing strategy is not going to help if you cannot implement it. When you have finished your marketing strategy, it is worth checking that you have the processes capable of fulfilling the extra orders, delivering on time and providing any extra services reliably and efficiently. It can be quite damaging for your reputation if you create all this buzz but cannot fulfil the demand you attract.

END

I hope this book has given you a clearer and firm foundation to become the great student entrepreneur that the world needs. In the next section of the book there is a comprehensive collection of resources to help you along with all the personal development and business knowledge gained in this book.

The final thought I would like to leave you with is this. You can have all the information in the world right in your hand. "NONE OF THE SUCCESS PRINCIPLES IN THIS BOOK WILL WORK IF YOU DON'T WORK."

PART 3
RESOURCES

SALES AND MARKETING

Organisations

The Chartered institute of Marketing (CIM)
Moor Hall, Cookham
Maidenhead
Berkshire SL6 9QH
01628 427500
www.cim.co.uk
A membership organisation for marketing professionals. Their website is a useful resource with downloadable documents on topics such as copyright, data protection, and so on. An online marketing plan 'tool' takes you through the creation of your own marketing plan.

Chartered institute of Public Relations
32 St James's square
London SW1Y 4JR
020 7766 3333
www.cipr.co.uk
Find a PR services provider, locate a PR consultant or professional body, or advertise your business using PR Directory.

Data Protection Registration
Information Commissioner's office
Wycliffe House Water Lane
Wilmslow, Cheshire SK9 5AF
08456 30 60 60
www.ico.gov.uk
Includes information to help you achieve compliance with the legislation, and publishes detailed guidance notes that provide all the information you need about electronic marketing.

Direct Marketing Association
www.dma.org.uk
Europe's largest trade association in the marketing and communications sector.

Direct Marketing Preference Services

Mailing Preference Service
DMA House
70 Margaret Street
London W1W 8SS
0845 703 4599
(MPS Registration line)
020 7291 3310
020 7323 4226
www.mpsonline.org.uk
Allows consumers to register their wish not to receive unsolicited direct mail.

- **The Email Preference Service**

Allows people to register an email address in order to not receive unsolicited sales and marketing email messages.
You can find information about having your email lists cleaned, or subscribe to this service at
www.dmaconsumers.org/emps.html

- **The Fax Preference Service**

Allows consumers and businesses to register their fax number/s in order to not receive unsolicited sales and marketing faxes.
www.fpsonline.org.uk

- **The Telephone Preference Service**

Allows businesses and consumers to registers their telephone numbers in order to not receive unsolicited sales and marketing calls.
www.tpsonline.org.uk

Direct Selling Association
29 Floral Street
London WC2E 9DP
020 7497 1234
ww.dsa.org.uk
Information and advice on the direct selling in the UK.

Experian
Business Strategies Division
www.business-strategies.co.uk
Mosaic UK is the latest version Experian's market-leading consumer segmentation product. It classifies all 24 million UK households into 11 groups, 61 types and 243 segments, and is updated each year. Click on 'Mosaic'

The Mail Order Traders Association
020 7735 3410
www.mota.org.uk

Market Research Society
15 Northburgh Street
London EC1V 0JR
020 7490 4911
020 7490 0608
www.mrs.org.uk
A membership organisation for professional researchers. You can search online their Research Buyer's Guide- a directory of market research providers / support services

Marketing Law
www.marketinglaw.co.uk
Regularly updated information for brand-owners and marketing professionals, including marketing and brand laws issues, case reports, legislation affecting marketing, as well as legal checklists and template agreements.

Books

Essential Marketing Sourcebook
Ros Jay and David Jay,
Financial Times Prentice Hall,
1998

Everything You Should Know About Public Relations: Direct Answers to Over 500 Questions
Anthony Davis
Kogan Page Ltd, 2003
Recommended for any small business doing its own PR.

Full Frontal PR:
Building Buzz About Your Business, Your Product, or You
Richard Laermer
Bloomberg Press, 2004

The Highly Effective Marketing Plan
Peter Knight, Financial Times
Prentice Hall, 2004
A process that will dramatically improve your chances of profitably selling more of your products and services.

How to exhibit at trade fairs
John Appleyard
How to Books, 2006
If you are considering exhibiting, this book will be invaluable. It covers everything from the planning stages, to getting the best out of your stand at the show, through to measuring the effectiveness of your campaign.

Market Research in Practice: A Guide to the Basics
Paul Hague, Nick Hague, Carol- Ann Morgan
Kogan Page Ltd, 2004
Describes the various tools and techniques available to

market researchers with practical advice and case studies.

Marketing Insights from A-Z
Phillips Kotler, John Wiley& Sons Inc, 2003
For a deeper understanding of marketing and how it fits together.

Marketing Judo- Building your business using brains not budget
John Barnes and Richard Richardson
Prentice Hall, 2002
A bestselling book that makes you think about all aspects of marketing.

The New Rules of Marketing & PR
David Meerman Scott
John Wiley & sons, 2007
How to use news release, blogs, podcasting , viral marketing and online to reach buyers directly

Power Networking and PR for Small Business
Moi Ali, Kogan Page Ltd, 1998
Addressing the needs of small businesses and those with limited budgets, this handbook provides full coverage of all aspects of marketing and PR.

Selling the invisible: A Field Guide to Morden Marketing
Harry Beckwith, Texere publishing, 2002
Bit- sized, practical, and intelligent strategies. Opens your eyes to new ideas that enhance the value and profitability of any company in today's service-orientated market.

Successful Marketing for the small business: A Practical Guide
Dave Patten, Kogan Page, 2001
This practical guide demonstrates how any service- or product- led organisation can be revitalised through basic

grasp of marketing.

The way of the Dog: The art of making success inevitable
Geoff Burch
Capstone, 2005
An off-the-wall approach to improving your chances of getting what you want from life and work.

Online Resources

Building Brands
www.buildingbrands.com
An excellent site by a UK company to help you learn about the benefits of building your own particular brand.
Free e-newsletter, 'Branding Tips'.

MarketingFile.com
www.marketingfile.com
Provides direct marketing data and services in the UK and Europe.

Marketing Law
www.marketinglaw.co.uk
Keeps you up-to-date with all aspects of legislation relating to marketing.

National Statistics Online
www.statistics.gov.uk
Free access to data produced by the Office for National Statistics

Survey Monkey
www.surveymonkey.com
A useful tool for creating professional online surveys quickly and easily.

Willings Press Guide
www.willingspress.com
Media directory with the reputation as the 'PR Bible' ; three print volumes or accessible online

Design resources

- **Fonts**

Font Pool
www.fontpool.com
Search by category and type.

Fonts.com
www.fonts.com
A wide range of PC & Mac fonts.

- **Photolibraries**

Comstock Images
www.comstock.com
A wide range of images

Eye Wire
www.eyewire .com
Portal site to Digital Vision, Image club, Rubberball, Photodisc

Getty Images
www.gettyimages.com
A wide range of high quality images

iStockphoto
www.istockphoto.com
A fabulous source of low-cost royalty- free images.

Photos.com
www.photos.com
One payment, unlimited downloads.

Rubberball
www.rubberball.com
A stylish and unusual mix of images

FINANCE

Accountants

ACCA (Association of Chartered Certified Accountants)
Central Quay
89 Hydepark Street
Glasgow G3 8BW
0141 582 2000
www.acca.org.uk
International body for accountants. ACCA also provides advice on choosing and accountant and you can search online for an ACCA member or an ACCA business advisor.

Banking Code Standards Board
Level 12, City Tower,
40 Basinghall Street,
London, EC2V 5DE
0845 230 9694
www.bankingcode.org.uk
The role of the BCSB is to monitor compliance with the building codes and to ensure subscribers provide a fair deal to their personal and small business customers. Download a free copy of the business banking code.

British Bankers' Association
Prinners Hall
105-107 Old Broad Street
London EC2N 1EX
www.bba.org.uk
The BBA, the voice of the banking industry, provides BankFacts, downloadable guides designed to provide an overview of selected banking products and services.
Written in plain language.

Institute of Chartered Accountants (England & Wales)
Chartered Accountants' Hall
PO Box 433, London EC2P 2BJ
020 7920 8682
www.icaew.co.uk
Online directory of chartered accountants and FAQs relating to running a small business.

Institute of Chartered Accountants of Scotland (ICAS)
CA House, 21 Haymarket Yards
Edinburgh EH12 5BH
0131 347 0100
www.icas.org.uk

Banks

Abbey National Business Banking
www.abbey.com

Alliance & Leicester
www.alliance-leicestercommercialbank.co.uk

Bank of Scotland
www.bankofscotland.co.uk

Barclays
www.clearlybusiness.co.uk

HBOS (Halifax/Bank of Scotland)
www.hbosplc.com

HSBC
www.ukbusiness.hsbc.com

Lloyds TSB
www.lloydstsb.com
www.success4business.com

NatWest
www.natwest.com

The Royal Bank of Scotland
www.rbs.co.uk

Grants and equity

The Asset Based Finance Association (ABFA)
Boston House, The Little Green Richmond, Surrey TW9 1QE
020 8332 9955
www.thefda.org.uk
A trade association; members provide factoring, invoice discounting and asset-based lending to UK businesses. The site contains a search box to help organisations looking for funding.

The British Venture Capital Association (BVCA)
3 Clements Inn
London WC2A 2AZ
020 7025 2950
www.bvca.co.uk
Represents over 400 private equity and venture capital

firms. They have produced a Guide to Private Equity aimed at entrepreneurs considering private equity and venture capital as an option for raising investment.
Available as a free download from their website.

Department for Business Enterprise And Regulatory Reform (BERR) *(previously DTI)*
Small Firms Loan Guarantee
www.berr.gov.uk
The SFLG guarantees loans from the banks and other financial institutions for small firms that have viable business proposals but who have tried and failed to get a conventional loan because of lack of security.

Finance and Leasing Association
2nd Floor, Imperial House
15-19 Kingsway
London WC2B 6UN
020 7836 6511
www.fla.org.uk
The industry body for asset finance.

Grantfinder
Enterprise House
Carlton Road, Worksop
Nottinghamshire S81 7QF
01909 501200
www.grantfinder.co.uk
Grantfinder advises and guides both industrial and professional clients on all matters relating to grant aid- from identifying what is available to whom, through to making application.

Grant Guide
www.grant-guide.com
Aimed at businesses, public sector organisations and their advisers, Grant-guide.com is designed to help users find the best form of funding for them.

J4b
www.j4bgrants.co.uk
Register to search for information about grants within your area or market sector. You are sent regular updates of any new information/grant available. An excellent resource.

National Business Angels Network (NBAN)
52-54 Southwark Street
London SE1 1UN
www.nban.co.uk
A trade association representing the UK's Business Angel Networks. Established in 1999, NBAN 'can help identify the right investors with the right management and skills while protecting confidentiality and commercial interests'.

Taxation

Chartered Institute of Taxation (CTA, ATII,FTII)
12 Upper Belgrave Street
London SW1X 8BB
020 7235 9381
www.tax.org.uk
The professional body for Chartered Tax Advisors; can help you find one in your area.

Corporation Tax
A general guide to corporation Tax Self- Assessment is free from the CTSA Orderline on
0845 300 6555.

HM Revenue & Customs
National Advice Service (VAT)
0845 010 9000
www.hmrc.gov.uk

New employer's helpline
0845 607 0143
www.hmrc.gov.uk

Registration helpline for self-employment
0845 9154 515

Online resources

Association of British Insurers
www.abi.org.uk

Banking Liaison Group
www.bankexperts.co.uk
Provides a professional service to UK businesses in getting business finance at good terms and providing advices on disputes and other banking issues.

Better Payment Practice Group
www.payontime.co.uk
Website promoting good payment practice among UK businesses. You can sign up to a code of practice.

Business Link
0845 600 9006
www.businesslink.gov.uk
Business Link is an easy to use business support, advice and information service managed by BERR, Free downloadable publications such as 'A User's Guide to late payment legislation' and many more best practice guides.

ChargeChecker
www.chargechecker.co.uk
Business software to help you to check your bank charges.

Department for Business Enterprise, Regulatory and reform (BERR)
(previously DTI)
www.berr.gov.uk
Information/signposting on sources of finance for small businesses.

Financial Ombudsman Service
www.financial-ombusman.org.uk
Provides consumers with a free independent service for solving disputes with financial firms.

Her Majesty's Courts Service
www.hmcourts-service.gov.uk
Forms and links to related guidance. Money Claim online is the Courts Service's site for making or responding to a money claim.
www.moneyclaim.gov.uk

Insolvency Service
www.insolvency.gov.uk
Deals with insolvency matters in England and Wales. The Redundancy Payments Service is part of The Insolvency Service and deals with redundancy and associated payments in England, Scotland and Wales.

MoneyFacts
www.moneyfacts.co.uk
An independent and unbiased website helping you make informed decisions on your finances.

PEOPLE

Organisations

ACAS (Advisory, Conciliation and Arbitration Service)
Brandon House
180 Borough High Street
London SE1 1LW
www.acas.org.uk

ACAS Helpline
08457 47 47 47

Minicom users
08457 47 47 47
(Formerly REAS- Race and Equality Advisory Service)

ACAS publications
08702 42 90 90
ACAS is the employment relations service that offers practical, independent and impartial advice to employers, employees and their representatives. The site has clear and useful leaflets and booklets, often free and most downloadable.

Apprenticeships
0800 150 400
www.apprenticeships.org.uk
Funded by the LSC, provides information on how apprenticeships can benefit businesses.

Basic Skills Agency at NIACE
Commonwealth House
1-19 New Oxford Street
London WC1A 1NU
020 7405 4017
www.basic-skills.co.uk
The Basic Skills Agency(BSA) has merged with the National Institute of Adult Continuing Education (NIACE) and will work in alliance with Tribal.

Benefits Enquiry Line
0800 882200

British Chambers of Commerce
65 Petty France
London SW1H PEU
020 7654 5800
www.chamberonline.co.uk

British Dyslexia Association
98 London Road, Reading
Berkshire RG1 5AU
0118 966 2677
www.bdadyslexia.org.uk
Help and advice for employers of staff with dyslexia.

Business Link
0845 600 9006
www.businesslink.gov.uk
Impartial advice for small businesses. The information is presented in factsheets, case studies, interactive tools and frequently- asked questions with links to other websites.

Centre foe Effective Dispute Resolution (CEDR)
020 7536 6000
www.cedr.co.uk

Chartered Institute of Personnel and Development (CIPD)
151 The Broadway
London SW19 1JQ
020 8612 6200
www.cipd.co.uk
The professional organisation for the management and development of people.

City & Guides
1 Giltspur Street
London EC1A 9DD
020 7294 2800
www.city-and-guilds.co.uk
The leader provider of vocational qualifications in the UK.

Criminal Records Bureau
0870 90 90 811
www.crb.gov.uk
Helps organisations in the public, private and voluntary sectors by identifying candidates who may be unsuitable to work with children or other vulnerable members of society.

Department for Business, Enterprise and Regulatory (BERR) *(previously DTI)*
Ministerial Correspondence
Unit, 1 Victoria Street
London SW1H OET
020 7215 5000
www.berr.gov.uk
A valuable source of information and advice for businesses of all sizes.

BERR Publications Orderline
0845 015 0010
www.berr.gov.uk

Department of Work and Pensions

1-11 John Adam Street
London WC2N 6HT
020 7712 2171
www.dwp.gov.uk
Information on services and benefits for people of working age, including those starting a business.

Department for Children, Schools and Families
0870 000 2288
www.dfes.gov.uk/employers
Information about apprenticeships, numeracy and literacy in the workplace, and training young people.

Disability Rights Commission
FREEPOST MID02164
Stratford upon Avon CV37 9BR
0845 7622 633
0845 7622 644 (Textphone)
www.drc-gb.org
An independent body set up by the Government to help eliminate discrimination against disabled people and to promote equality of opportunity. The site contains wealth resource information.

Edexcel- Training
One90 High Holborn
London WC1V 7BH
0870 240 9800
www.edexcel.org.uk
Part of Pearson plc, Edexcel is the UK's largest awarding body and offers a range of both general and specialist qualifications, including both BTEC short courses and work-based National Vocational Qualifications (NVQs).

Employment Agencies Standards Inspectorate
1 Victoria Street
London SW1H OET
08459 555 105
The regulation employment agencies is undertaken by the Employment Agency Standards Inspectorate of the Department for Business, Enterprise and Regulatory Reform (BERR).

Employment Tribunals
(Enquiry Line)
0845 795 9775

Equality Direct
0845 600 3444
www.equalitydirect.org.uk
An ACAS telephone advice service and supporting website for business, offering authoritative, confidential and down-to-earth advice about equality issues.

Health & Safety Executive (HSE)
All enquiries relating to occupational health and safety should be directed to the HSE infoline:
Rose Court
2 Southwark Bridge
London SE1 9HS
0845 345 0055
0845 408 9577 (Minicom)

HSE Publication
PO Box 1999, Sudbury
Suffolk C010 2WA
01787 881 165
www.hsebooks.co.uk

HM Revenue & Customs
Employer's Helpline
08457 143 143
www.hmrc.gov.uk/employers

Investors in People
7-10 Chandos Street
London W1G 9DQ
020 7467 1900
www.investorsinpeople.co.uk
The national standard that sets a level of good practice for training and development of people to achieve business goals.

The Learning and Skills Council
LSC helpdesk 0870 900 6800
www.ls.gov.uk
The LSC is committed to improvement of the further education and training sector to raise standards and to make learning provision more responsive to the needs of individuals and employers.

Learn Direct
08000 150 750
www.learndirect-business.co.uk
Courses and training for business owners and employees. Learn direct also offer a series of Directors' Briefings on such subjects as: appraisal, training, leadership, managing change.

National Minimum Wage
Helpline: 0845 6000 678

The Pensions Regulator
Napier House, Trafalgar Place
Brighton BN1 4DW
0870 6063636
www.thepensionsregulator.gov.uk
The regulator of work-based pension schemes in the UK. Provides assistance and guidance to employers. The site contains useful information for employers about stakeholder pensions and their implementation.

Sector Skills Development Agency
3 Callflex Business Park
Wath-upon-Dearne
South Yorkshire S63 7ER
www.ssda.org.uk
The Sector Skills Development Agency (SSDA) funds, supports and champions the new UK-wide network of employer-led Sector Skills Councils (SSCs).

Trades Union Congress (TUC)
Great Russell Street
London WC1B 3LS
020 7636 4030
www.tuc.org.uk
The TUC website directory is a superb resource for employers alike on such topics as health and safety, the law, equality and learning.

Train to Gain
0800 015 55 45
www.traintogain.gov.uk
The Learning and Skills Council's Train to Gain service provides impartial, independent advice on training to businesses across England.

Working Links
Garden House
57-59 Long Acre
Covent Garden
London WCE 9JL
0800 91790 262
www.workinglinks.co.uk
Gets the long-term unemployed back to work, and helps them stay there by matching people looking for work with businesses with recruitment needs.

Online resources

Employing Migrant Workers
www.employingmigrantworkers.org.uk
If you currently employ staff from outside the UK, or are planning to, you're legally required to make checks on their right to work here. This Home Office site provides a step-by-step guide to check someone is entitled to work in the UK.

TIGER (Tailored Interactive Guidance on Employment Rights)
www.tiger.gov.uk
The ACAS user-friendly guide to different aspects of UK employment law. An excellent resource with a wealth of information including the national minimum wage, flexible working rights, and tools to help you work out maternity, paternity and adoption rights.

Workplace Law
www.workplacelaw.net
Provides free (and subscription) employment law information for employers (registration necessary).

WorkSmart

www.worksmart.org.uk

A TUC site that covers everything you need to know about being a responsible employer including many aspects of health and safety in the workplace and employees' rights. An invaluable resource.

Your People Manager

www.yourpeoplemanager.com

A free service that helps owners of small businesses to deal with the everyday questions, issues and problems of managing staff.

Books

Managing People in a Small Business

John Stredwick

Kogan Page Ltd, 2002

Key topics: recruitment and selection, improving performance training and development, rewarding employees, legal considerations, and disciplining and dismissing staff.

The Employer's Handbook: An Essential Guide to Employment Law, Personnel Policies and Procedures

Barry Cushway

Kogan Page Ltd, 2007

A comprehensive, reliable and affordable source of guidance

The A to Z of Work

Provides a brief introduction to important employee relations topics; gives basic information on a number of subjects and where appropriate, gives references to further sources of guidance.

Ref: ACAS/H03

Employing People: Handbook for Small Firms

Provides an introduction to the business of employing

people in small firms. Primarily for organisations without specialist personnel expertise. Deals essentially with the employment of 'employees', but organisations of all sizes may well employ other types of workers, for instance, casual, agency-supplied temporary, home workers and so on. Ref: ACAS/H01

LEGAL

Companies House
Crown Way, Maindy
Cardiff CF14 3UZ
0879 333 3636
www.companieshouse.gov.uk
All limited companies in the UK are registered at Companies House.

Data Protection Registration
The Information Commissioner's Office
Wycliffe House, Water Lane
Wilmslow, Cheshire SK9 5AF
08456 30 60 60
www.ico.gov.uk
Information to help you achieved compliance with the legislation.

Department for Business Enterprise and Regulatory Reform (BERR) *(previously DTI)*
Ministerial Correspondence
Unit, 1 Victoria Street
London SW1H OET
020 7215 5000
www.berr.gov.uk

A valuable source of information and advice for businesses of all sizes.

Disability Rights Commission
FREEPOST MID02164
Stratford upon Avon CV37 9BR
0845 7622 633
0845 7622 644 (Textphone)
www.drc.org.uk
Information about making goods and services accessible to disabled people.

Health & Safety Executive (HSE)
Rose Court, 2 Southwark Bridge
London SE1 9HS
0845 345 0055
0845 408 9577 (Minicom)
www.hse.gov.uk

Institute of Chartered Secretaries and Administrators (ICSA)
16 Park Crescent
London W1B 1AH
020 7580 4741
www.icsa.org.uk
Provides advice on the role of being a Company Secretary in a limited company.

Law Society of England & Wales
The Law Society's Hall
113 Chancery Lane
London WC2A 1PL
020 7242 1222
www.lawsociety.org.uk

Law society of Northern Ireland
40 Linenhall Street
Belfast BT2 8BA
028 90 231614
www.lawsoc-ni.org

Lawyers For Your Business Scheme
020 7405 9075
www.lawsociety.org.uk
A scheme, run by The Law Society, in which solicitors who are members offer half an hour's free basic legal consultation for businesses.

National Solicitors' Network
0845 3889 0381
www.tnsn.com
Can help you find the right solicitor for your business.

Office of Fair Trading (OFT)
Fleetbank House
2-6 Salisbury Square
London EC4Y 8JX
08457 22 44 99
www.oft.gov.uk
Explanations of some of the laws that might affect you.

Patents and IP

The European Patent Office
www.epo.org
Provides a uniform application procedure for individual inventors and companies seeking patent protection in up to 37 European countries.

Institute of Patentees and Inventors
PO Box 39296
London SE3 7WH
0871 226 2091
www.invent.org.uk
Offers members advice and guidance on all aspects of inventing.

Institute of Trade Mark Attorneys
2-6 Sydenham Road
Croydon, Surrey CRO 9XE
020 8686 2052
www.itma.org.uk
A professional body for attorneys specialising in trade mark matters.

UK Copyright Service
www.copyrightservice.co.uk
Registers original works by artists, musicians, designers, software providers, authors and many other organisations and individual.

UK Intellectual Property Office
Concept House
Cardiff Road, Newport
South Wales NP10 8QQ
0845 9 500 505
www.patent.gov.uk
The essential first point of contact for any enquiries to do with trademarks of patents.

Online resources

Connecting Legal
www.chambersdirectory.co.uk
Helps people find the appropriate legal professional or service.

Solicitors- Online
www.lawsociety.org.uk
A link within The Law Society website to find a solicitor in the UK.

Tribunals Service (Employment)
www.employmenttribunals.gov.uk
Information on employment tribunals, including the process for making a claim and the latest Rules of Procedure.

Waterlow Legal
www.chambersdirectory.co.uk
Helps people find the appropriate legal professional or service.

Anti-virus and malware protection

Business Link
0845 600 9006
www.businesslink.gov.uk
A comprehensive guide to IT, Suppliers, systems, software and eCommerce. With useful interactive tools to help you implement the right technology for tour business and minimise the IT risks.

The Business Software Alliance (BSA)
2 Queen Anne's Gate Buildings
Dartmouth Street
London SW1 H9BP
0207 340 6080

www.bsa.org/uk
The BSA provides guidelines on how to manage your business software. You can download from their website a guide to software management and free software audit tools.

Department for Business, Enterprise & Regulatory Reform (BERR) *(previously DTI)*
www.berr.gov.uk
Provides IT guides with detailed regulatory and other legal information for people starting businesses and for larger companies.

Data Protection

Information Commissioner's Office
Wycliffe House
Water Lane, Wilmslow
Cheshire SK9 5AF
08456 30 60 60
www.ico.gov.uk
Download or order free, a wide range of guides and training materials covering data protection and the freedom of information to achieve information Security best practice in your business.

Scotland
Scottish information Commissioner
www.itspublicknowledge.info

Domain names

Nominet
Stranford Gate
Sandy Lane West
Oxford OX4 6LB

01865 332244
www.nic.uk
The organisation that looks after UK internet (co.uk) addresses.

InterNIC
www.internic.net
For other internet addresses.

eCommerce

Direct Marketing Association
www.dma.org.uk
Europe's largest trade association in the marketing and communications sector.

Health and safety

HSE Publications
01787 881 165
www.hse.gov.uk/pubns/index.htm
Free leaflets on many topics including: Working with VDUs, RSI, Upper limb disorders (including Aching arms in smack businesses). Available online or to order as print copies.

Security

The Department for Business, Enterprise & Regulatory Reform (BERR)
Has an online health-check tool to assess how secure your business is at:
www.securityhealthcheck.berr.gov.uk
It also has extensive documentation, including the useful

information: Security: Protecting Your Business Assets. Download a guide on information Security that details how to assess and manage digital risks:
www.berr.gov.uk/files/file9971.pdf

Federation Against Software Theft
www.fast.org.uk
Information on software piracy and licensing.

Fraud Advisory Panel
www.fraudadvisorypanel.org
Free guides (Cybercrime- what every SME should know and Fighting fraud- a guide for SME's) advise on the types of fraud to look out for. They can be downloaded from the Publications section of the Fraud Advisory Panel site.

Janet-Cert
www.ja.net/cert/threats
Keep up to date with the latest security issues and problems at the UK's education and research network.

Online Community

Blogs
Detailed information on blogs is available from www.thefreesite.com/Free_Blog_Resources

Book: **Blog WILD! How everyone can go blogging.**
Andy Wibbels
Nicholas Brealey Publishing, 2006
A great starting point for small business professionals who want to become bloggers.

Wiki
The is a wealth of online resources about Wikis. Good places to start are www.wiki.com , www.wiki.org

Open source

The Free Software Foundation
www.fsf.org
This site has a Free Software Directory that catalogues useful free software that runs under free operating systems.

Open Source Initiative (OSI)
www.opensource.org
Find out more about open source software from this non-profit corporation.
SourceForge
http://sourceforge.net/
SourceForge.net is the World's largest Open Source Software development website, with more than 100,000 projects.

Operating system updates

Updates are free from the website of the company that created your system:
For Windows XP, Choose Control Panel from the Start menu, then open Automatic Updates.
For MAC OS X, choose Software Update from the Apple menu, and allow the instructions
For Linux, visit your distribution's web page.

Search engine optimisation (SEO)

SearchEngineWatch
http://searchenginewatch.com
Search Engine Watch provides tips and information about searching the web, analysis of the search engine industry and help to site owners trying to improve their ability to be found in search engines.

Wordtracker
www.wordtracker.com
One of the best places to research keyword frequency

Website usability and accessibility

These resources are useful for people who are new to the topic and appreciate a simple checklist to compare their website with. These are some of the easily understandable ones, which are supported by research:

Accessibility 101
www.accessibility101.org.uk
Accessibility 101 is a collection of FAQs, research, findings, UK laws and recommendations concerning accessible website design in the UK.

HiSoftware
www.cynthiasays.com
A good general testing tool for simple usability/accessibility checks

IBM Ease of Use Group
www.03.ibm.com/easy
Guidelines on using a user-centered design process so that businesses can retain current customers and attract new ones. Follow the links to the Design area.

Jakob Niesen's website
www.useit.com
Information and links from 'the king of usability'

Quality Framework for UK Government Website Design
http://archive.cabinetoffice.gov.uk/e-government/resources/quality-framewok.asp

For government web managers, but useful for other web managers. Pulls together advice from a wide range of web publishers, usability experts, designers, web managers and academics to clarify what relevant usability and design criteria should be used when planning a website or judging how good it is.

Royal National Institute of the Blind (RNIB)
www.rnib.org.uk
A free online resource called the Web Access Centre provides help on making your site accessible to people with disabilities.

Stanford Persuasive Technology Lab
www.webcredibility.org/guidelines
Ten easy-to-follow guidelines, based in research, for building the credibility of a website

Sun Microsystems
www.sun.com/980713/webwriting
'Writing for the Web' guidelines can be used to help make sites easy to read and navigate.

The Web Accessibility Initiative (WAI)
www.w3.org/WAI
WAI pursues accessibility of the web through technology, guidelines, tools, education, and research and development. The WAI is part of The World Wide Web Consortium (W3C). The W3C's Web Content Accessibility Guidelines, guidelines are relevant to usability as well as accessibility, and are the standards recommended by the UK government.

Plus
Many websites provide free and simple usability and accessibility checks. A good general testing tool is at www.cynthiasays.com
There is also information on making your site more accessible

to Deaf people at: www.accessiblity101.org.uk

MANAGING YOUR BUSINESS

Exporting

British Chambers of Commerce
www.chamberonline.co.uk/exportzone
The 'exportzone' on the BCC website contains the 'information, advice and links you need to turn your export potential into export successes.

BSI British Standards
www.mysmallbiz.co.uk
Sign up to receive free access to the quarterly Business Standards magazine.

The Institute of Export
Export House
Minerva Business Park
Lynch Wood
Peterborough, PE2 6FT
01733 404400
www.export.org.uk
Specialises in helping you complete your international trade transactions

Simplifying International Trade Ltd
020 7215 8150
www.sitpro.org.uk
Dedicated to encouraging and helping businesses to trade more effectively and to simplifying the international trading process

UK Trade & Investment
Kingsgate House
66-74 Victoria Street
London SW1E 6SW
020 7215 8000
www.uktradeinvest.gov.uk
The Government organisation that supports companies in the UK trading internationally and oversees

Franchising

British Franchise Association
www.thebfa.org
The professional body that oversees the UK franchise industry. Runs seminars for people thinking of franchising their own businesses

Franchise for Sale
www.FranchiseForSale.com
Website with worldwide franchise opportunities

Green business

The Carbon Trust
8th Floor, 3 Clement's Inn
London WC2A 2AZ
Energy Helpline
0800 085 2005
www.thecarbontrust.co.uk/energy
Free advice on reducing your energy costs and waste management. Download free the Better Business Guide to Energy Saving- a quick and easy guide to identifying energy saving opportunities in your business.

Egeneration
www.egeneration.co.uk
egeneration is a new resource in the fight for sustainable business, providing services, best practice advice and support, for free.

Environment Agency UK
08708 506 506
www.environment-agency.gov.uk
The public body for protecting and improving the environment in England and Wales

Envirowise
0800 585 794
www.envirowise.gov.uk
Free, independent, confidential advice and support on practical ways to increase profits, minimise waste and reduce environmental impact.

Freecycle
www.freecycle.org
Discover your local Freecycle group and give stuff away; you'll reduce waste, save precious resources and ease the burden on landfill sites.
Friends of the Earth
020 7490 1555
www.foe.co.uk
Briefing papers on recycling and legislation requirements.

Greenbiz
www.greenbiz.com
Looks at such things as computer and paper recycling, how to make your building environmentally efficient.

NetRegs Environment Agency
Block 1, Government Buildings

Burghill Road, Westbury-on-Trym,
Bristol, BS10 6BF
08708 506 506
www.netregs.gov.uk
Free environmental guidance for small businesses to help you understand what you need to do to comply with environmental legislation and protect the environment.

Scottish Environment Protection Agency (SEPA)
SEPA Corporate Office
Erskine Court
Castle Business Park
Stirling FK9 4TR
01786 457700
www.sepa.org.uk
Guidance on protecting the environment in Scotland

Small Business Journey Business in the Community
137 Shepherdess Walk
London N1 7RD
020 7566 6653
www.smallbusinessjourney.com
How small businesses can realise more value by behaving responsibly. Download the Better Business Journey, a jargon-free guide for SMEs full of tips and practical actions for businesses to increase their profitability and responsibility.

Sustainable Development Unit (part of the Department for Environment, Food and Rural Affairs- DEFRA)
www.sustainable-development.gov.uk
Corporate social responsibility- applied to working practices today- offers businesses an opportunity to innovate as well as benefit from cost reductions. Follow the 'Taking the lead' boxes on the advice for business pages.

UK Green Power
www.ukgreenpower.co.uk

A free service to compare prices on green energy tariffs

Waste Electrical and Electronic Equipment Detective (WEEE)
020 7238 4344
www.defra.gov.uk/envoironment/waste/topics/electrical
Aims to reduce the quantity of waste from electrical and electronic equipment and increase its re-use, recovery and recycling. DEFRA is responsible for permitting Authorised Treatment Facilities for the WEEE Directive.

Waste Watch
56-64 Leonard Street
London EC2A 4JX
020 7549 0300
www.wastewatch.org.uk
Information on waste reduction

Other Organisations

British Chambers of Commerce
65 Petty France
London SW1H 9EU
020 7654 5800
www.chamberonline.co.uk
Local chambers seek to represent the interests and support the competitiveness and growth of all businesses in their communities and regions.

British Insurance Brokers Association (BIBA)
14 Bevis Marks
London EC3A 7NT
0901 814 0015
www.biba.org.uk
An independent insurance body.

British Quality Foundation
32-34 Great Peter Street
London SW1P 2QX
020 7654 5000
www.quality-foundatin.co.uk
A not-for-profit membership organisation that promotes business excellence.

Business in the Community
137 Shepherdess Walk
London N1 7RQ
0870 600 2482
www.bitc.org.uk
The aim is 'to inspire, challenge, engage and support business in continually improving its positive impact on society'.

Business Link
0845 600 9006
www.businesslink.gov.uk
Business Link is an easy to use business support, advice and information service managed by BERR. Free downloadable advice and interactive tools for running your business on a day-to-day basis.

CBI
Centre Point
103 New Oxford Street
London WC1A 1DU
020 7379 7400
www.cbi.org.uk
A lobbying organisation for UK businesses to help create the conditions in which businesses can thrive.

Department for Innovation, universities and Skills (DIUS)
0870 0010 336
www.dius.gov.uk

Brings together the nation's strengths in science, research, universities and colleges to build a dynamic, knowledge-based economy.

Directors' Briefings BHP Information Solutions
Althorpe House
4-6 Althorpe Road
London SW17 7ED
020 8672 6844
www.bhpinfosolutions.co.uk
A wide range of practical business information and advice for small and medium-sized enterprises (SMEs).

Eureka
020 7215 1681
www.eureka.be
Useful if your business wants to find a European partner to share the technological, financial and commercial risk in the development of new products or services.

Institute for Small Business and Entrepreneurship
2nd Floor, 3 Ripon Road
Harrogate, HG1 2SX
01423 500046
www.isbe.org.uk
Membership organisation for researchers and policy makers.

Institute of Directors
116 Pall Mall
London SW1Y 5ED
020 7839 1233
www.iod.com
A membership organisation for company directors, providing information, advice, training, conferences and publications.

Institute of Leadership and Management

1 Giltspur Street
London EC1A 9DD
020 7294 2470
www.i-l-m.com
Offers members and accredited centres the opportunity to invest in leadership and management competencies and skills.

Knowledge Transfer Partnerships
0870 190 2829
www.ktponline.org.uk
Can help a business to develop and grow by accessing the knowledge and expertise in the UK's universities, colleges and research organisations.

Opportunity Wales
Venture House
Navigation Park, Abercynon
Rhondda Cynon Taf CF45 4SN
0845 8500 888
www.opportunitywales.co.uk
A non-profit partnership supporting the development of e-commerce in small and medium-sized businesses.

The Prince's Trust
18 Park Square East
London NW1 4LH
0800 842 842
www.princes-trust.org.uk
Provides loans and grants to young people aged between 18 and 30 years old who want to start or develop their own business.

SFEDI- Small Firms Enterprise Development Initiative
01234241255
www.sfedi.co.uk
Government-recognised to research and disseminate what works best for small businesses. The website offers free advice on products and services to help you develop your business.

Trade Association Forum
103 New Oxford Street,
London WC1A 1DU
www.taforum.org
Encourages the development and sharing of best practice among UK trade associations. Comprehensive links to information on UK trade associations.

Trade Standards
www.tradingstandards.gov.uk
Advice that relates to specific regulations for different industries to ensure you are trading under the right licences.

Online resources

The Bag Lady
www.the-bag-lady.co.uk
Aims to be a comprehensive directory where women can find other women in business when they need a service or product. Women business owners can add their listing to the directory free of charge.

Bizhelp24
www.bizhelp24.com
Offers business financial resources throughout the UK.

Ecademy
www.ecademy.com
An online business exchange that connects people to knowledge, contacts, support and business.

e-Co
www.e-co.co.uk
Provides an online business club that offers members a ready-made community of businesses with which they can trade, discuss issues and access business support online.

EnterpriseQuest
www.enterprisequest.com
On this site, you can read EnterQuest, the weekly tips and ideas bulletin, or you can subscribe and have it sent to you by e-mail.

Everywoman
www.everywoman.co.uk
An online network and resource provider for women business owners and managers.

Freelancers in the UK
www.freelancersintheuk.co.uk
Provides help and information on freelancing plus a list of freelancers in the UK.

Your Hidden Potential
http://yourhiddenpotential.co.uk
A website that gathers inspirational stories about entrepreneurs.

ABOUT THE AUTHOR

Junior Ogunyemi is a multi-award winning "student entrepreneur" who became a business starlet while studying for a BSc in Economics at Queen Mary University. By graduation, he owned a football coaching academy operating in schools and communities across London, launched a publishing company that produced several magazines and ran numerous other ventures. For the past 7 years, he has dedicated his time to studying & shadowing renowned millionaires from around the globe. In this book he shares lessons learned and useful tips to help you make your own fortune before you graduate.

He is now a full-time social entrepreneur and inspirational speaker. The central theme of his message is life transformation and maximization of individual potential. He is the founder and president of the Bold Achievers Club. (www.boldachievers.com). He is also the founding director of Show Me Amazing football, (www.smafootball.com)a coaching academy that uses sports as a vehicle to develop leadership and excellence in young children.

Awards & Honours

- Voted in the top 10 most outstanding black students in the UK for 2010 by Rare Rising Stars
- Winner of the 2010 NACUE national varsity pitch award for social enterprise
- Winner of the 2010 BYA award for Business and Enterprise
- Winner of the Unltd Sport Relief Award
- Winner of the Knowledge East Enterprise Network award

Network with Junior:
www.boldachievers.com/profile/JuniorOgunyemi

Like the page on Facebook:
How To Be A Student Entrepreneur

Follow him on twitter:
@JuniorOgunyemi

Subscribe on YouTube:
boldachiversclub

Lightning Source UK Ltd.
Milton Keynes UK
UKOW020746081111

181666UK00002B/25/P